VICTORY OVER VICE

&

THE SEVEN VIRTUES

FULTON J. SHEEN

Bishop Sheen Today
280 John Street
Midland, Ontario, Canada
L4R 2J5
www.bishopsheentoday.com

Library of Congress Cataloging-in-Publication Data

Names: Sheen, Fulton J. (Fulton John), 1895-1979, author. | Smith, Allan J., editor.

Sheen, Fulton J. (Fulton John), 1895-1979. Victory Over Vice. - Registered in the name of P.J. Kenedy & Sons, under Library of Congress catalog card number: A 128052, following publication April 13, 1939.

Sheen, Fulton J. (Fulton John), 1895-1979. The
Seven Virtues. - Registered in the name of P.J.
Kenedy & Sons, under Library of Congress catalog
card number: A139984 following publication April
26, 1940.

Title: Victory Over Vice & The Seven Virtues
Fulton J. Sheen; compiled by Allan J. Smith.

Description: Midland, Ontario: Bishop Sheen
Today, 2021

Includes bibliographical references.

Identifiers:
ISBN: 978-1-998229-23-9 (paperback)
ISBN: 978-1-990427-70-1 (hardcover)
ISBN: 978-1-990427-60-2 (eBook)

Subjects: Jesus Christ — The Seven Last Words —
The Seven Deadly Sins — The Seven Virtues

Second Printing

J.M.J.

DEDICATED TO

Mary Immaculate Mother of God

IN TOKEN OF FILIAL
GRATITUDE AND AFFECTION.

IN HUMBLE PETITION WE PRAY
FOR THE GRACE
TO PRACTICE THE VIRTUES
AND FOR
VICTORY OVER VICE

Ad maiorem Dei gloriam
inque hominum salutem

Jesus calls all His children to the pulpit of the Cross, and every word He says to them is set down for the purpose of an eternal publication and undying consolation.

There was never a preacher like the dying Christ.

There was never a congregation like that which gathered about the pulpit of the Cross.

And there was never a sermon like the Seven Last Words.

Archbishop Fulton J. Sheen

THE SEVEN LAST WORDS OF CHRIST

The First Word
"Father, Forgive Them For They

Know Not What They Do."

The Second Word
"This Day Thou Shalt Be With Me In Paradise."

The Third Word
"Woman, Behold Thy Son;

Behold Thy Mother."

The Fourth Word
"My God! My God!

Why Hast Thou Forsaken Me?"

The Fifth Word
"I Thirst."

The Sixth Word
"It Is Finished."

The Seventh Word
"Father, Into Thy Hands I Commend My Spirit."

CONTENTS

PREFACE

"I have learned more from the
crucifix than from any book."
St. Thomas Aquinas

ARCHBISHOP FULTON J. SHEEN was a man
for all seasons. Over his lifetime, he spent
himself for souls, transforming lives with the
clear teaching of the truths of Christ and His
Church through his books, his radio addresses,
his lectures, his television series, and his many
newspaper columns.

The topics of this much-sought-after
lecturer ranged from the social concerns of the
day to matters of faith and morals. With an easy
and personable manner, Sheen could strike up
a conversation on just about any subject,
making numerous friends as well as converts.

During the 1930s and '40s, Fulton Sheen
was the featured speaker on The Catholic Hour
radio broadcast, and millions of listeners heard

his radio addresses each week. His topics ranged from politics and the economy to philosophy and man's eternal pursuit of happiness.

Along with his weekly radio program, Sheen wrote dozens of books and pamphlets. One can safely say that through his writings, thousands of people changed their perspectives about God and the Church. Sheen was quoted as saying, "There are not one hundred people in the United States who hate the Catholic Church, but there are millions who hate what they wrongly perceive the Catholic Church to be."

Possessing a burning zeal to dispel the myths about Our Lord and His Church, Sheen gave a series of powerful presentations on Christ's Passion and His seven last words from the Cross. As a Scripture scholar, Archbishop Sheen knew full well the power contained in preaching Christ crucified. With St. Paul, he could say, "For I decided to know nothing among you except Jesus Christ and him crucified" (1 Cor. 2:2).

During his last recorded Good Friday address in 1979, Archbishop Sheen spoke of having given this type of reflection on the subject of Christ's seven last words from the Cross "for the fifty-eighth consecutive time." Whether from the young priest in Peoria, Illinois, the university professor in Washington, D.C., or the bishop in New York, Sheen's messages were sure to make an indelible mark on his listeners.

Given their importance and the impact they had on society, it seemed appropriate to bring back this collection of Sheen's radio addresses that were later compiled into two books titled *Victory over Vice* (New York: P.J. Kenedy and Sons, 1939) and *The Seven Virtues* (New York: P.J. Kenedy and Sons, 1940)

On October 2, 1979, when visiting St. Patrick's Cathedral in New York City, Pope John Paul II embraced Fulton Sheen and spoke into his ear a blessing and an affirmation. He said: "You have written and spoken well of the Lord Jesus Christ. You are a loyal son of the Church." On the day Archbishop Sheen died (December 9, 1979), he was found in his private chapel before the Eucharist in the shadow of the cross. Archbishop Sheen was a man purified in the fires of love and by the wood of the Cross.

It is hoped that, upon reading these reflections, the reader will concur with the heartfelt affirmation given by St. John Paul II and countless others of Sheen's wisdom and fidelity.

May these writings by Archbishop Fulton J. Sheen evoke in us a greater love and understanding of how the Seven Last Words can be used as a remedy to help one overcome the seven deadly sins of anger, envy, lust, pride, gluttony, sloth, and covetousness.

And may these Seven Last Words also provide us with that same encouragement to practice the seven virtues of Fortitude, Hope, Prudence, Faith, Temperance, Justice, and Charity.

VICTORY

OVER VICE

FULTON J. SHEEN

INTRODUCTION TO VICTORY OVER VICE

THESE MEDITATIONS ON the Seven Last Words correlated to the seven deadly sins make no pretence to absoluteness. The Words are not necessarily related to the seven deadly sins but they do make convenient points of illustrations.

This book has only one aim: to awaken a love in the Passion of Our Lord and to give the reader encouragement in winning a victory over one, or many, of the seven deadly sins. If it does that in but one soul, its publication has been justified.

ANGER

*"Father, forgive them, for they
know not what they do."*

THE ONE PASSION IN man that has deeper
roots in his rational nature than any other is the
passion of anger. Anger and reason are capable
of great compatibility because anger is based
upon reason, which weighs the injury done and
the satisfaction to be demanded. We are never
angry unless someone has injured us in some
way — or we think he has.

But not all anger is sinful, for there is
such a thing as just anger. The most perfect
expression of just anger we find in Our Blessed
Lord's cleansing of the Temple. Passing
through its shadowed doorways at the festival
of the Pasch, He found greedy traders,
victimizing at every turn the worshippers who
needed lambs and doves for the temple
sacrifices.

Making a scourge of little cords He moved through their midst with a calm dignity and beautiful self-control even more compelling than the whip. The oxen and sheep He drove out with His scourge; with His Hands, He upset the tables of the money changers who scrambled on the floor after their rolling coins; with His finger, He pointed to the vendors of doves and bade them leave the outer court; to all He said: "Take these things hence, and make not the house of my Father a house of traffic."

Here was fulfilled the injunction of the Scriptures, "Be angry, and sin not," for anger is no sin under three conditions: 1 — If the cause of anger be just, for example, defense of God's honor; 2 — If it is no greater than the cause demands, that is, if it is kept under control; and 3 — If it is quickly subdued: "Let not the sun go down upon your anger."

Here we are not concerned with just anger, but with unjust anger, namely, that which has no rightful cause — anger which is excessive, revengeful, and enduring; the kind of anger and hatred against God that has destroyed religion on one-sixth of the earth's surface; and which recently in Spain burned 25,000 churches and chapels and murdered 12,000 servants of God: the kind of hatred which is not only directed against God, but also against fellowman, and is fanned by the disciples of class conflict who talk peace but glory in war; the red anger which rushes the blood to the surface, and the white anger which pushes it to the depths and bleaches the face; the anger that seeks to "get even", to repay in kind, bump for bump, punch for punch, eye for eye, lie for lie; the anger of the clenched fist prepared to strike, not in defense of that which is loved but in offense against that which is hated; in a word, the kind of anger that will destroy our civilization unless we smother it by love.

Our Blessed Lord came to make reparation for the sin of anger, first by teaching us a prayer: "Forgive us our trespasses as we forgive those who trespass against us"; and then by giving us a precept: "Love your enemies; do good to them that hate you." More concretely still, He added, "Whosoever will force thee one mile, go with him another two ... if a man ... take away thy coat, let go thy cloak also unto him."

Revenge and retaliation were forbidden: "You have heard that it has been said: an eye for an eye, and a tooth for a tooth. But I say unto you, Love your enemies." These precepts were made all the more striking because He practiced them.

When the Gerasenes became angry at Him because He put a higher value on an afflicted man than on a herd of swine, Scripture records no retort: "And entering into the boat, He passed over the water." To the soldier who struck Him with a mailed fist, He meekly responded: "If I have spoken evil, give testimony of the evil, but if well, why strikest thou me?"

The perfect reparation for anger was made on Calvary. We might also say that anger and hate led Him up that hill. His own people hated Him, for they asked for His crucifixion; the law hated Him, for it forsook justice to condemn Justice; the Gentiles hated Him for they consented to His death; the forests hated Him for one of its trees bore the burden of His weight; the flowers hated Him as they wove thorns for His brow; the bowels of the earth hated Him as it gave its steel as hammer and nails.

Then as if to personalize all that hatred, the first generation of clenched fists in the history of the world stood beneath the Cross and shook them in the face of God. That day they tore His body to shreds as in this day they smash His tabernacle to bits. Their sons and daughters have shattered crucifixes in Spain and Russia as they once smote the Crucified on Calvary.

Let no one think the clenched fist is a phenomenon of the twentieth century; they whose hearts freeze into fists today are but the lineal descendants of those who stood beneath the Cross with hands lifted like clubs against Love as they hoarsely sang the first International of hate.

As one contemplates those clenched fists, one cannot help but feel that if ever anger would have been justified, if ever Justice might have fittingly judged, if ever Power might have rightfully struck, if ever Innocence might have lawfully protested, if ever God might have justly revenged Himself against man — it was at that moment.

And yet, just at that second when a sickle and a hammer combined to cut down the grass on Calvary's hill to erect a cross, and drive nails through hands to render impotent the blessings of Love incarnate, He, like a tree which bathes in perfume the axe which kills it, let's fall from His lips for the earth's first hearing the perfect reparation for anger and hate — a prayer for the army of clenched fists, the First Word from the Cross: "Father, forgive them, for they know not what they do."

The greatest sinner may now be saved; the blackest sin may now be blotted out; the clenched fist may now be opened; the unforgivable may now be forgiven. While they were most certain that they knew what they were doing, He seizes upon the only possible palliation of their crime and urges it upon His Heavenly Father with all the ardor of a merciful Heart: ignorance — "they know not what they do." If they did know what they were doing as they fastened Love to a tree, and still went on doing it, they would never be saved. They would be *damned.*

It is only because fists are clenched in ignorance that they may yet be opened into folded hands; it is only because tongues blaspheme in ignorance that they may yet speak in prayer. It is not their conscious wisdom that saves them; it is their unconscious ignorance.

This Word from the Cross teaches us two lessons: 1 — The reason for forgiving is ignorance; and 2 — There are no limits to forgiveness.

The reason for forgiving is ignorance. Divine Innocence found such a reason for pardon; certainly, guilt can do no less. St. Peter's first Pentecostal sermon used this very excuse of ignorance for the Crucifixion so fresh in his mind: "The author of life you killed . . . and now, brethren, I know that you did it through ignorance, as did also your rulers."

If there were full consciousness of the evil, perfect deliberation, perfect understanding of the consequences of acts, there would be no room for forgiveness. That is why there is no redemption for the fallen angels. They knew what they were doing. We do not. We are very ignorant — ignorant of ourselves and ignorant of others.

Ignorant of others! How little we know of their motives, their good faith, the circumstances surrounding their actions. When others visit violence upon us, we too often forget how little we know about their hearts and say: "I cannot see that they have the slightest excuse; they knew very well what they were doing." And yet in exactly the same circumstances, Jesus found an excuse: "They know not what they do."

We know nothing about the inside of our neighbor's heart, and hence we refuse to forgive. He knew the heart inside out, and because He did know, He forgave. Take any scene of action, let five people look upon it, and you will get five different stories of what happened. No one of them sees all sides. Our Lord does, and that is why He forgives.

Why is it that we can find excuses for our anger against our neighbor, and yet we refuse to admit the same excuses when our neighbor is angry with us? We say others would forgive us if they understood us perfectly, and that the only reason they are angry with us is because "they do not understand."

Why is not that ignorance reversible? Can we not be as ignorant of their motives, as we say they are ignorant of ours? Does not our refusal to find an excuse for their hatred tacitly mean that under similar circumstances, we ourselves will be unfit to be forgiven?

Ignorance of ourselves is another reason for forgiving others. Unfortunately, it is ourselves we know least; our neighbor's sins, weaknesses, and failures we know a thousand times better than our own. Criticism of others may be bad, but it is want of self-criticism, which is worse.

It would be less wrong to criticize others if we first criticized ourselves, for if we first turned the searchlight into our own souls, we would never feel we had a right to turn it on the soul of anyone else. It is only because we are ignorant of our true condition that we fail to realize how badly we stand in need of pardon.

Have we ever offended God? Has He any right to be angry with us? Then why should we, who need pardon so badly, strive not to purchase it by pardoning others? The answer is because we never examine our own consciences.

We are so ignorant of our true condition that we know little more of ourselves than our name and address and how much we have; of our selfishness, our envy, our detraction, our sin, we know absolutely nothing. In fact, in order that we may never know ourselves, we hate silence and solitariness. Lest our conscience should carry on with us an unbearable repartee, we drown out its voice in amusements, distractions, and noise. If we met ourselves in others, we would hate them.

If we knew ourselves better, we would be more forgiving of others. The harder we are on ourselves, the easier we will be on others; the man who has never learned to obey knows not how to command, and the man who has never disciplined himself knows not how to be merciful.

It is always the selfish who are unkind to others, and those who are hardest on themselves are the kindest to others, as the teacher who knows the least is always the most intolerant to his pupils.

Only a Lord who thought so little of Himself as to become man and die like a criminal could ever forgive the weakness of those who crucified Him.

It is not hatred that is wrong; it is hating the wrong thing that is wrong. It is not anger that is wrong; it is being angry at the wrong thing that is wrong. Tell me your enemy, and I will tell you what you are. Tell me your hatred, and I will tell you your character.

Do you hate religion? Then your conscience bothers you. Do you hate the capitalists? Then you are avaricious, and you want to be a capitalist. Do you hate the laborer? Then you are selfish and a snob. Do you hate sin? Then you love God. Do you hate your hate, your selfishness, your quick temper, and your wickedness? Then you are a good soul, for "If any man come to me . . . and hate not his own life, he cannot be my disciple."

The second lesson to be derived from this First Word from the Cross is that there is no limit to pardon. Our Lord forgave when He was innocent and not because He Himself had been forgiven. Hence we must forgive not only when we have been forgiven, but even when we are innocent.

The problem of the limits of pardon once troubled Peter, and He asked our Lord: "How often shall my brother offend against me, and I forgive him till seven times?" Peter thought he was stretching forgiveness by saying "seven times," for it was four more than the Jewish Masters enjoined.

Peter proposed a limit beyond which there was to be no forgiveness. Peter assumed the right to be forgiven is automatically renounced after seven offenses. It is equivalent to saying, "I renounce my right to collect debts from you if you never owe me more than seven dollars, but if you exceed that sum, then my duty of further cancellation ceases. I can throttle you for eight dollars."

Our Lord, in answering Peter says that forgiveness has no limits; forgiveness is the surrender of all rights and the denial of limits. "I say not to thee till seven times but till seventy times seven." That does not mean 490 literally, but infinitely. The Saviour then proceeded to tell the parable of the unjust steward who immediately after being forgiven by his lord a debt of 10,000 talents, choked a fellow servant who owed him a hundred pence. The unmerciful steward by refusing to be merciful to his debtor had his own mercy revoked. His guilt was not that, needing mercy he refused to show it, but having received mercy, he was unmerciful still. "So also shall my heavenly Father do to you if you forgive not everyone his brother."

Forgive then, and we will be forgiven; remit our anger against others and God will remit His anger against us. Judgment is a harvest where we sow what we reap. If we sowed anger against our brethren during life, we will reap the just anger of God. Judge not, and we shall not be judged.

If, during life, we forgive others from our hearts, on Judgment Day the All-Wise God will permit something very unusual to Himself: He will forget how to add and will know only how to subtract. He who has a memory from all eternity will no longer remember our sins. Thus, we will be saved once again through Divine "Ignorance."

By forgiving others on the ground that they know not what they do, Our Lord will forgive us on the ground that He no longer remembers what we did. It may well be that if He looks on a hand that, now after hearing the first Word on the Cross gives a kindly blessing to an enemy, He will even forget that it was once a clenched fist red with the blood of Christendom.

"And dars't thou venture still to live in sin,
And crucify thy dying Lord again?

Were not His pangs sufficient? Must he bleed
Yet more? O, must our sinful pleasures feed
Upon his torments, and augment the story
Of the sad passion of the Lord of glory!

Is there no pity? Is there no remorse
In human breasts? Is there a firm divorce

Betwixt all mercy and the hearts of men?
Parted for ever – ne'er to meet again?

No Mercy bides with us: 'tis thou alone,
Hast it, sweet Jesus, for us, that have none

For thee: thou hast forestall'd our markets so
That all's above, and we have none below:

Nay, blessed Lord, we have not wherewithal
To serve our shiftless selves: unless we call

To thee, thou art our Saviour, and hast power
To give, and whom we crucify each hour:

We are cruel, Lord, to thee and ourselves too;
Jesus forgive us; we know not what we do."

Francis Quarle

ENVY

"This day thou shalt be with me in paradise."

ENVY IS SADNESS AT another's good, and joy at another's evil. What rust is to iron, what moths are to wool, what termites are to wood, that envy is to the soul: the assassination of brotherly love.

We are not here concerned with just envy or zeal which inspires us to emulate good example and to progress with those who are our betters, for the Scriptures enjoin us to "be zealous for spiritual gifts"; rather, we here touch on that sinful envy which is a wilful grieving at another's good, either spiritual or temporal, for the reason that it seems to diminish our own good. The honor paid to another is regarded by the envious man as a reflected disgrace on himself, and he is sad in consequence. Envy manifests itself in discord, hatred, malicious joy, back-biting, detraction, imputing of evil motives, jealousy, and calumny.

A sample of this kind of envy we find in one of the two women who asked Solomon to adjudicate their dispute. The first woman said, "I and this woman dwelt in one house . . . And this woman's child died in the night: for in her sleep, she overlaid him. And rising in the dead time of the night, she took my child from my side while I thy handmaid was asleep . . . and laid her dead child in my bosom. "To which the other woman answered: "It is not so as thou sayest, but thy child is dead, and mine is alive."

Since there were no witnesses, Solomon ordered a sword to be brought to him, for he rightly judged that the motherly heart of the real mother would rather give up her child than see it killed. Brandishing the glittering sword, he said, "Divide the living child in two, and give half to the one, and half to the other." Hearing this, the woman whose child was alive cried out in terror and pity, "I beseech thee, my lord, give her the child alive, and do not kill it." But the other said, "Let it be neither mine nor thine, but divide it."

Then the king commanded the child be given to her who would rather give it up to another than have it killed, knowing that she must be the mother. The point of the story is that envy, which is so jealous of the good of another, may reach a point where it scruples not to take a life.

In our times, envy has taken on an economic form. The avarice of the rich is being matched by the envy of the poor. Some poor hate the rich not because they have unjustly stolen their possessions, but because they want their possessions. Certain *have-nots* are scandalized at the wealth of the *haves*, only because they are tempted by lust for their possessions.

The Communists hate the Capitalists only because they want to be Capitalists themselves; they envy the rich, not because of their need, but because of their greed.

Combined with this is social envy or snobbery which sneers at the higher position of others because the snobs want to sit in their chairs and enjoy their applause. They assume that in not arriving at such popular favor themselves they were deprived of their due. That is why we hate those who do not pay sufficient attention to us and why we love those who flatter us.

If envy is on the increase today, as it undoubtedly is, it is because of the surrender of the belief of a future life and righteous Divine Justice. If this life is all, they think they should have all. From that point on, envy of others becomes their rule of life.

Our Lord was unceasing in His preaching against envy. To those who were envious of the mercy extended to lost sheep, He pictured the angels of Heaven rejoicing more at the one sinner doing penance than at the ninety-nine just who needed not penance. To those who were envious of wealth, He warned: "Lay not up to yourselves treasures on earth: where the rust and moth consume, and where thieves break through and steal. But lay up to yourselves treasures in heaven: where neither the rust nor moth consume and where thieves do not break through, nor steal."

To those who were envious of power, such as the Apostles quarreling about first place, He placed a child in the midst of them and, "putting His arms around him" reminded them that heaven was open only to those who were as simple children, for Christ is not in the great but in the little: "Whosoever shall receive one such child as this in my name, receiveth me. And whosoever shall receive me, receiveth not me, but him that sent me."

But His preaching against envy did not save Him from the envious. Pilate was envious of His power; Annas was envious of His innocence; Caiphas was envious of His popularity; Herod was envious of His moral superiority; the Scribes and Pharisees were envious of His wisdom. Each of these had built his judgment seat of mock moral superiority from which to sentence Morality to the Cross. And in order that He might no longer be a person to be envied, they reputed Him with the wicked.

Born between an ox and an ass, they now crucify Him between two criminals. That was the last insult they could give Him. To the public eye, they created the impression that three thieves and not two were silhouetted against the sky. In a certain sense, it was true: two stole gold out of avarice; one stole hearts out of love. *Salvandus, Salvator,* and *Salvatus*: The thief who could have been saved; the thief who was saved; and the Saviour who saved them. The crosses spelled out the words Envy, Mercy, and Pity.

The thief on the left envied the Power which Our Blessed Lord claimed. As the chief priests, scribes, and ancients ridiculed the Saviour, sneering: "He saved others — himself he cannot save," the thief on the left added to their revilings: "If Thou be Christ, save thyself and us." In other words: "If I had that power of yours, that power which you claim as the Messiah, I would use it differently than to hang helpless on a tree. I would step down from the Cross, smite my enemies, and prove what power really is."

Thus did Envy reveal that if it had the gifts which it envies in others, it would misuse them, as the thief on the left would have surrendered redemption from sin for release from a nail. In like manner, many in the world today who are envious of wealth would probably lose their souls if they had that wealth. Envy never thinks of responsibilities. Looking only to self it misuses every gift that comes its way.

Pity has quite a different effect on the soul. The thief on the right had no envy of the Master's Power but only pity for the Master's sufferings. Rebuking his companion on the left, the good thief said: "Neither dost thou fear God, seeing thou art under the same condemnation? And we indeed, justly, for we receive the due reward of our deeds; but this man hath done no evil."

There was not a spark of envy in him. He wanted nothing in all the world, not even to be removed from tragic companioning with his cross. He was not envious of God's Power, for God knows best what to do with His Power. He was not envious of his fellowmen, for they had nothing worth giving.

So he threw himself upon Divine Providence and asked only for forgiveness: "Lord, remember me when thou shalt come into thy kingdom." A dying man asked a dying Man for life; a man without possessions asked a Poor

Man for a Kingdom; a thief at the door of death asked to die a thief and steal Paradise. And because He envied nothing, He received all: "Amen, I say to thee, this day thou shalt be with me in Paradise."

One would have thought a saint would have been the first soul purchased over the counter of Calvary by the red coins of redemption, but in the Divine plan, it is a thief who steals that privilege and marches as the escort of the King of Kings into Paradise.

Two lessons are taught us by this Second Word from the Cross. The first is that envy is the source of our wrong judgments about others. The chances are that if we are envious of others, nine times out of ten, we will misjudge their characters.

Because the thief on the left was envious of the Power of Our Lord, he misjudged Him and missed both the Divinity of the Saviour and his own salvation. He falsely argued that Power should always be used the way he would have used it, namely to turn nails into rosebuds, a cross into a throne, blood into royal purple, and the blades of grass on the hillside into bayonets of offensive steel.

No one in the history of the world ever came closer to Redemption, and yet no one ever missed it so far. His envy made him ask for the wrong thing; he asked to be taken down when he should have asked to be taken up. It makes one think of how much the envy of Herod resulted in an equally false judgment: He massacred the Innocents because He thought the Infant King came to destroy an earthy kingdom, whereas He came only to announce a heavenly one.

So it is with us. Backbiting, calumny, false judgments, are all born of our envy. We say, "Oh, he is jealous," or "she is jealous"; but how do we know that he or she is jealous unless we ourselves have felt that way? How do we know others are acting proudly unless we know how pride asserts itself? Every envious word is based on a false judgment of our own moral superiority. To sit in judgment makes us feel that we are above those who are judged and more righteous and more innocent than they.

To accuse others is to say: "I am not like that." To be envious of others is to say: "You have stolen that which is mine." Envy of others' wealth has resulted in the gross misjudgment that the best way to do away with its abuse in the hands of the rich is to dispossess them violently, so that the dispossessors may in their turn, enjoy its abuse.

Envy of others' political power has given rise to the erroneous philosophy that even governments may be overthrown if organized violence is strong enough to do so.

Envy thus becomes the denial of all justice and love. In individuals, it develops a cynicism that destroys all moral values, for by bankrupting others do we ourselves become bankrupt. In groups, it produces a deceit that extends the glad hand of welcome to those who differ, only until they are strong enough to cut it off.

Since envy is so rampant in the world today, it is extremely good counsel to disbelieve 99/100 percent of the wicked statements we hear about others. Think of how much the thief on the right had to discount to arrive at the truth. He had to disbelieve the judgment of four envious judges, the raillery of envious scribes and ancients, the blasphemous utterances of curious onlookers who loved murders, and the envious taunts of the thief on the left who was willing to lose his soul if only he could keep his fingers nimble for more thefts.

But if he had been envious of the Lord's power, he would never have been saved. He found peace by disbelieving the envious scandalmongers. Our peace is found in the same incredulity.

The chances are that there is a bit of jealousy, a bit of envy, behind every cutting remark and barbed whispering we hear about our neighbor. It is always well to remember that there are always more sticks under the tree that has the most apples. There should be some consolation for those who are so unjustly attacked to remember that it is a physical impossibility for any man to get ahead of us who stays behind to kick us.

A second lesson to be learned from this Word is that the only way to overcome envy is, like the thief on the right, to show pity. As

Christians in good faith, we are all members of the Mystical Body of Christ and should, therefore, love one another as Christ has loved us.

If our arm suffers an injury, our whole body feels the pain. In like manner, if the Church in any part of the world suffers martyrdom, we should feel pity toward it as part of our body, and that pity should express itself in prayer and good works. Pity should be extended not only to those outside the Church who are living as if the earth never bore a Cross but even to the enemies of the Church who would destroy even the shadow of the Cross. God is their Judge; not we.

And as potential brothers of Christ, sons of a Heavenly Father and children of Mary, they must be worth our pity since they were worth the Saviour's Blood. Unfortunately, there are some who blame the Church for receiving great sinners into the Church on their deathbeds.

A few years ago one who was generally believed to be a racketeer and murderer met death at the hands of his fellow criminals. A few minutes before his death, he asked to be received into the Church, was baptized, received First Communion, and was anointed and given the last blessing. Some who should have known better protested against the Church. Imagine! Envy at the salvation of a soul!

Why not rather rejoice in God 's Mercy, for after all did he not belong to the same profession as the thief on the right — and why should not Our Lord be just as anxious to save twentieth-century thieves as first-century thieves? They both have souls. It would seem that sinful envy of the salvation of a thief is a greater sin than thievery.

One thief was saved: therefore let no one despair. One thief was lost: therefore let no one presume. Have pity then on the miserable, and Divine Mercy will be the reward for your pity. When the Pharisees accused Our Lord of eating with publicans and sinners, He retorted by reiterating the necessity of mercy: "The healthy have no need of a physician, but the sick have. Now go and learn what this means; *I will have mercy and not sacrifice*. For I am not come to call the just, but sinners."

One day a woman went to the saintly Father John Vianney, the Curé of Ars, in France, and said: "My husband has not been to the sacraments or to Mass for years. He has been unfaithful, wicked, and unjust. He has just fallen from a bridge and was drowned — a double death of body and soul." The Curé answered: "Madam, there is a short distance between the bridge and the water, and it is that distance which forbids you to judge. "

There was just that distance between the two crosses which saved the penitent thief. If the thief on the right had been self-righteous, he would have looked down on Jesus and lost his soul. But because he was conscious of his own sin, he left room for Divine Pardon.

And the answer of the Redeemer to his request proves that to the merciful, love is blind — for if we love God and our neighbor, who may even be our enemy, Divine Love will go blind as it did for the thief on the right. Christ will no longer be able to see our faults, and that blindness will be for us the dawn of the vision of Love.

THE PENITENT THIEF

"Say, bold but blessed thief,
That in a trice
Slipped into paradise,

And in plain day
Stol'st heaven away,
What trick couldst thou invent
To compass thy intent?

What arms?
What charms?"
"Love and belief."
"Say, bold but blessed thief,

How couldst thou read
A crown upon that head?
What text, what gloss –
A kingdom and a cross?
How couldst thou come to spy
God in a man to die?
What light?
What sight?"

"The sight of grief —"
"I sight to God his pain;
And by that sight
I saw the light,

Thus did my grief
Beget relief.
And take this rule from me,
Pity thou him he'll pity thee.

Use this,
Ne'er miss,
Heaven may be stolen again."

Anonymous

LUST

"Woman, behold thy son.
. . . behold thy mother."

LUST IS AN INORDINATE love of the pleasures of the flesh. The important word here is *inordinate* for it was Almighty God Himself who associated pleasure with the flesh. He attached pleasure to eating in order that we might not be remiss in nourishing and preserving our individual lives; He associated pleasure with the marital act in order that husband and wife might not be remiss in their social obligations to propagate mankind and raise children for the Kingdom of God.

The pleasure becomes sinful at that point where, instead of using it as means, we begin to use it as an end. To eat for the sake of eating is a sin because eating is a means to an end, which is health. Lust, in like manner, is selfishness or perverted love.

It looks not so much to the good of the other, as to the pleasure of self. It breaks the glass that holds the wine; it breaks the lute to snare the music. It subordinates the other to self for the sake of pleasure. Denying the quality of "otherness," it seeks to make the other person care for us, but not to make us care for the other person.

We are living today in what might properly be called an era of carnality. As the appeal to the spiritual relaxes, the demands of the flesh increase. Living less for God, human nature begins to live only for self, for "no man can serve two masters: For either he will hate the one, and love the other: or he will sustain the one, and despise the other."

Peculiar to this era of carnality is the tendency to equate the perpetuity of marriage with the fleshly pleasure so that when the pleasure ends the bond is presumed to be automatically dissolved. In America, for example, there is more than one divorce for every four marriages — an indication of how much we have ceased to be a Christian nation and how much we have forgotten the words of Our Lord: "What therefore God hath joined together, let no man put asunder."

The regrettable aspect of it all is that with this increased sin there is a decreased sense of sin. Souls sin more but think less about it. Like sick who are so moribund that they have no desire to be better, sinners become so calloused they have no yearning for redemption. Having lost their eyes, they no longer want to see; the only pleasure left them, in the end, is to mock and sneer at those who do.

It is never the pure who say that chastity is impossible, but only the impure. We judge others by ourselves and attribute to others the vices from which we ourselves refuse to abstain.

Some reparation had to be made for the sin of lust which in Old Testament times became so hideous to God that He would have withheld the destruction of the cities of Sodom and Gomorrah could but ten just men have been found within their gates.

Our Lord began making reparation for it at the first moment of the Incarnation for He chose to be born of a virgin. Why did He choose to transcend the laws of nature? The answer is very simple. Original Sin has been propagated to every human being from Adam to this very hour, with the exception of Our Lady. The prolongation of this taint in human nature takes place through the carnal act, of which man is the active principle, for man was the head of the human race. Every time there is generation of one human being by another, through the union of man and woman, there is the propagation of original sin.

The problem confronting the Second Person of the Blessed Trinity in becoming man was: how become man without at the same time becoming sinful man, that is, man-infected by the sin to which all flesh is heir? How to become man without inheriting original sin? He had to be a true man in order to suffer for man, but He could not be a sinful man if He were to redeem man from sin. How could He be both man and yet sinless?

He could be man by being born of a woman; He could be sinless man, without original sin, by dispensing with man as the active principle of generation — in other words, by being born of a virgin. Thus it was that when the Angel Gabriel appeared to Mary and told her that she was to conceive the Messias whose name would be called Jesus, she answered: "How can this be done because I know not man?" She had made the vow of virginity, and she intended to keep it.

The Angel answered that the conception of the Son of Man would take place without man, through the power of the Holy Ghost who would overshadow her. Being assured of her continued virginity, she accepted the motherhood of God Incarnate. "Be it done unto me, according to thy word."

So it was that reparation for sins of the flesh began the first moment of the Incarnation through the Virgin Birth. That same love He manifested for virginity, in the beginning, He re-echoed in the first sermon of His public life: "Blessed are the clean of heart: for they shall see God."

Later on, to the Scribes and Pharisees who sought to malign His good name, He challenged them to find anything impure in His life: "Which of you shall convince me of sin?"

The final atonement and reparation is made on Calvary where, in reparation for all the impure desires and thoughts of men, Our Lord is crowned with thorns; where, in reparation for all the sins of shame, He is stripped of His garments; where, in reparation for all the lusts of the flesh, He is almost dispossessed of His flesh, for according to Sacred Scripture, the very bones of His Body could be numbered.

We are so used to looking upon artistic crucifixes of ivory and the beautiful images in our prayer books, that we think of Our Blessed Lord as being whole on the Cross. The fact is that He made such reparation for sins of the flesh that His Body was torn, His Blood poured forth, and Scripture refers to Him on the Cross as a leper, as one struck by God and afflicted, so that "there is no beauty in Him, nor comeliness . . . that we should be desirous of Him."

Our Lord chose to go even further in reparation for the sins of lust by dispossessing Himself of the two most legitimate claims of the flesh. If there was ever a pure and legitimate claim in the realm of the flesh, it is the claim to the love of one's own Mother. If there is any honest title to affection in the universe of the flesh, it is the bonds of love that attach one to a fellow man. But the flesh was so misused by man and so perverted that Our Divine Saviour renounced even these legitimate bonds of the flesh in order to atone for the illegitimate.

He became totally un-fleshed, in order to atone for the abuse of the flesh, by giving away His Mother and His best friend. So, to His own Mother, He looks and bids farewell: "Woman, behold thy son"; and to His best friend He looks and bids farewell again: "Behold thy mother."

How different from the world! A mother will deprive her son of an advanced education in a foreign land, saying: "I cannot give up my son"; or a wife will deprive her husband of good material advancement through a short absence, saying: "I cannot give up my husband." These are not the cries of noble love but of attachment. Our Lord did not say: "I cannot give up My Mother." He gave her up. He loved her enough to give her away for her life's plan and destiny, namely, to be *our* Mother.

Here was a love that was strong enough to forget itself, in order that others might never want for love. He made the sacrifice of His Mother that we might have her; He wounded Himself like the pelican, that we might be nourished by her motherhood. Mary accepted the poor exchange to carry out her Son's redemptive work. And at that moment when Jesus surrendered even the legitimate claims of the flesh and gave us His Mother, Mary, and His best friend, John — selfishness died its death.

Two lessons are to be learned from this Third Word from the Cross:

1 — The only real escape from the demands of the flesh is to find something more than the flesh to love; and 2 — Mary is the refuge of sinners.

If we could ever find anything we loved more than the flesh, the demands of the flesh would be less imperative. This is the "escape" a mother offers her boy when she says: "Don't do anything of which your mother would ever be ashamed." If there is that higher love of his mother, the boy will always have a consecrated sense of affection, something for which he will be willing to make sacrifices.

When a mother makes such an appeal to her son, she is merely re-echoing the lesson of the Saviour, who, in giving His Mother to us as our Mother, equivalently said: "My children, never do anything of which your Mother would be ashamed." Let a soul but love that Mother and He will love her Divine Son Jesus, Who, in order to make satisfaction for the unlawful pleasure of the flesh, surrendered to us His last and lawful attachment — His Mother.

The psychology of this enthusiasm for a higher love of Jesus and Mary as an escape from the unlawful attachments of the flesh is this: by it, we avoid undue concentration on lower loves and their explosions. Think about your mouth for five minutes, and you will have an undue concentration of saliva. Think about your heart for five minutes and you will believe you have heart trouble, though the chances are nine out of ten that you have not. Stand on a stage and think about your hands and they will begin to feel as big as hams.

The balance and equilibrium of the whole system is disturbed when an organ is isolated from its function in the whole organism, or divorced from its higher purpose. Those people who are always talking, reading, and thinking about sex are like singers who think more about their larynx than about singing. They make that which is subordinate to a higher purpose so all-important that the harmony of life is upset.

But suppose that, instead of concentrating on an organ, one fitted that organ into a pattern of living — then all the uneasiness would end. The skilled orator never feels his hands are awkward because, being enthused about his speech, he makes his hands subordinate to their higher purpose.

Our Lord practically said the same thing: "Be not solicitous . . . what you shall eat." So it is with the flesh. Cultivate a higher love, a purpose of living, a goal of existence, a desire to correspond to all that God wants us to be, and the lower passion will be absorbed by it.

The Church applies this psychology to the vow of chastity. The Church asks her priests and nuns to surrender even the lawful pleasures of the flesh, not because she does not want them to love, but because she wants them to love better. She knows that their love for souls will be greater as their love for the flesh is less, just as Our Lord died on the Cross for men because He loved His Own life less.

Nor must it be thought that the vow of chastity is a burden. Thompson has called it a "passionless passion, a wild tranquility." And so it is. A new passion is born with the vow of chastity, the passion for the love of God. It is the consolation of that higher love which makes the surrender of the lower love so easy. And only when that higher love is lost does the vow begin to be a burden, just as honesty becomes a burden only to those who have lost the sense of others' rights.

The reason there is a degeneration in the moral order and a decay of decency is because men and women have lost the higher love. Ignoring Christ their Saviour, who loved them unto the death on Calvary, and Mary who loved them unto becoming Queen of Martyrs beneath that Cross, they have nothing for which to make the sacrifice.

The only way love can be shown in this world is by sacrifice, namely, the surrender of one thing for another. Love is essentially bound up with choice, and choice is a negation, and negation is a sacrifice. When a young man sets his heart upon a maid and asks her to marry

47

him, he is not only saying "I choose you"; he is also saying "I do not choose, I reject, all others. I give them all up for you." Apply this to the problem of lust.

Take away all love above the flesh, take away God, the crucifix, the Sorrowful Mother, salvation, eternal happiness — and what possibility is there for choice, what is to be gained by denying the imperious and revolutionary demands of the flesh? But grant the Divine, and the flesh's greatest joy is to throw itself on the altar of the one loved where it counts its sorrow a cheap price for the blissful joy of giving.

Then its greatest despair is not to be needed; it could almost find it in its heart to inflict a wound that it might bind and heal. Such is the attitude of the pure: they have integrated their flesh with the Divine; they have sublimated its cravings with the Cross; having a higher love, they now make the surrender of the lower, that their Mother may never be put to shame.

Mary is the refuge of sinners. She who is the Virgin Most Pure is also the Refuge of

Sinners. She knows what sin is, not by the experience of its falls, not by tasting its bitter regrets, but by seeing what it did to her Divine Son.

She looked upon His torn and bleeding flesh hanging from Him like rays of a purple sunset — and she came to know how much flesh sinned by seeing what His flesh suffered. What better way in all the world was there to measure the heinousness of sin than by seeing when left alone with Him for three hours, what it could do to Innocence and Purity.

She is the Refuge of Sinners not only because she knows sin through Calvary, but also because she chose, during the most terrifying hours of her life, a converted sinner as her companion. The measure of our appreciation of friends is our desire to have them about us in the moment of our greatest need.

Mary heard Jesus say, "The harlots and publicans will enter the Kingdom of Heaven before the Scribes and Pharisees." So she chose the absolved harlot, Magdalen, as her companion at the Cross. What the scandalmongers of that day must have said when they saw Our Blessed Mother in the company of a woman who everyone knew was the kind who sold her body without giving away her soul.

Magdalen knew that day why Mary is the Refuge of Sinners, and certainly our day, too, can learn that if she had Magdalen as a companion then, she is willing to have us as companions now.

Mary's purity is not a holier-than-thou purity, a stand-offish holiness that gathers up its robes lest they be stained by the sinful; nor is it a despising purity which looks down upon the impure. Rather, it is a radiating purity that is no more spoiled by solicitude for the fallen than a ray of sunshine is sullied by a dirty window pane through which it pours.

There is no reason for the fallen to be discouraged. Hope is the message of Golgotha. Find a higher love than the flesh, a love pure, understanding, redeeming, and the struggle will be easy. That higher love is on the Cross and beneath it.

We almost seem to forget that there is a Cross at all. He begins to look more like a red rose, and she begins to look like the stem. That stem reaches down from Calvary into all our wounded hearts of earth, sucking up our prayers and petitions and conveying them to Him. That is why roses have thorns in this life — to keep away every disturbing influence that might destroy our union with Jesus and Mary.

ACKNOWLEDGMENT

If Christ should come on earth some summer day
And walk unknown upon our busy street
I wonder how 'twould be if we should meet,
And being God — if He would act that way.

Perhaps the kindest thing that He would do
Would be just to forget I failed to pray
And clasp my hand, forgivingly, and say,
"My child, I've heard My Mother speak of you."

Mrs. Frederick V. Murphy

PRIDE

"My God, My God, why
hast thou forsaken me?"

PRIDE IS AN INORDINATE love of one's own excellence, either of body or mind or the unlawful pleasure we derive from thinking we have no superiors. Pride being swollen egoism, it erects the human soul into a separate center of origin apart from God, exaggerates its own importance, and becomes a world in and for itself. All other sins are evil deeds, but pride insinuates itself even unto good works to destroy and slay them. For that reason, Sacred Scriptures says, "Pride goeth before destruction."

Pride manifests itself in many forms: *atheism*, which is a denial of our dependence on God, our Creator and our final end; *intellectual vanity*, which makes minds unteachable because they think they know all there is to know; *superficiality*, which judges others by their clothes, their accent, and their bank account; *snobbery*, which sneers at inferiors as the earmark of its own superiority, "they are not of our set"; *vain-glory*, which prompts some Catholic parents to refuse to send their boys and girls to Catholic colleges, because they would there associate only with the children of carpenters; *presumptuousness*, which inclines a man to seek honors and positions quite beyond his capacity; and *exaggerated sensitiveness*, which makes one incapable of moral improvements because of unwillingness to hear one's own faults.

Pride it was that made Satan fall from Heaven and man fall from grace. By its very nature, such undue self-exaltation could be cured only by self-humiliation. That is why He who might have been born in a palace by the Tiber, as befitting His Majesty as the Son of God, chose to appear before men in a stable as a child wrapped in swaddling bands.

Added to this humility of His Birth was the humility of His profession — a carpenter in an obscure village of Nazareth whose name was a reproach among the great. Just as today there are those who sneer at the humble walks of life, so too, there were then those who sneered: "Is not this the carpenter's son?" There was also the humility of His actions, for never once did He work a miracle in His own behalf not even to supply Himself with a place to lay His head.

Humility of example there was too, when on Holy Thursday night, He who is the Lord of heaven and earth, girds Himself with a towel, gets down on His knees, and with basin and water, washes the twenty-four calloused feet of His Apostles saying: "The servant is not greater than his lord . . . If then I being your Lord and Master have washed your feet; you also ought to wash one another's feet." Finally, there was humility of precept: "Unless you be converted, and become as little children, you shall not enter into the kingdom of heaven."

But the supreme humiliation of all was the manner of death He chose, for "He humbled Himself . . . even to the death of the cross." To atone for false pride of ancestry, He thrusts aside the consolation of Divinity; for pride of popularity, He is laughed to scorn as He hangs cursed upon a tree; for pride of snobbery, He is put in the company of thieves; for pride of wealth, He is denied even the ownership of His own deathbed; for pride of flesh, He was scourged until "there was no beauty in Him"; for pride in influential friends, He is forgotten even by those whom He cured; for pride of power, He is weak and abandoned; for pride of those who surrender God and their Faith, He wills to feel without God.

For all the egotism, false independence, and atheism, He now offers satisfaction by surrendering the joys and consolations of His Divine Nature. Because proud men forgot God, He permits Himself to feel God-lessness, and it breaks His heart in the saddest of all cries: "My God, my God, why hast thou forsaken me?" There was union even in the separation, but they were words of desolation uttered that we might never be without consolation.

Two lessons emerge from this Word: 1 — Glory not in ourselves for God resists the proud; and 2 — Glory in humility for humility is truth and the path to true greatness.

Why should we be proud? As St. Paul reminds us, "Or what hast thou that thou hast not received? And if thou hast received, why dost thou glory, as if thou hadst not received it?" Is it our voice, our wealth, our beauty, our talents of which we are proud? But what are these but gifts of God, anyone of which He might revoke this second?

From a material point of view, we are worth so little. The content of a human body is equivalent to as much iron as there is in a nail, as much sugar as there is in two lumps, as much oil as there is in seven bars of soap, as much phosphorus as there is in 2200 matches, and as much magnesium as it takes to develop one photograph. In all, the human body, chemically, is worth a little less than two dollars — "O why should the spirit of mortal be proud?"

But *spiritually* we are worth more than the universe: "For what shall it profit a man, if he gains the whole world, and suffer the loss of his soul? Or what shall a man give in exchange for his soul?"

God resists the proud. The Pharisee who praised his own good deeds in the forefront of the Temple is condemned; the poor publican in the rear of the temple, who calls himself a sinner and strikes his breast in a plea for pardon, goes to his house justified. The harlots and the publicans who are conscious of their sin enter the kingdom of Heaven before the Scribes and the Pharisees, who are conscious of their righteousness.

The Heavenly Father is thanked for concealing His Wisdom from the self-wise and the conscious intellectuals and for revealing it to the simple: "I confess to thee, O Father, Lord of heaven and earth, because thou hast hidden these things from the wise and prudent and hast revealed them to little ones."

Surely anyone who has had experience with the proud will bear witness to the truth of this statement: If my own eternal salvation were conditioned upon saving the soul of one self-wise man who prided himself on his learning, or one hundred of the most morally corrupt men and women of the streets, I should choose the easier task of converting the hundred. Nothing is more difficult to conquer in all the world than intellectual pride. If battleships could be lined with it instead of with armor, no shell could ever pierce it.

This is easy to understand, for if a man thinks he knows it all, there is nothing left for him to know, not even what God might tell him. If the soul is filled to the brim with the ego, there is no place left for God. If a vessel is filled with water, it cannot also be filled with oil. So it is with the soul.

God can give His Truth and Life only to those who have emptied themselves. We must create a vacuum in our own souls to make room for grace. We live under the impression that we do more than we actually do. Take, for example, the simple fact of drinking liquid through a straw. We erroneously believe that we draw up the liquid through the straw. We do not, for strictly speaking there is no such thing as suction. All that we do is create a vacuum; the atmosphere presses down on the liquid with a weight equal to that of an ocean covering the earth to a depth of thirty-four feet. It is this pressure that pushes the liquid up through the straw when we create the vacuum.

So too in our spiritual lives. The good we accomplish is not through the action of ourselves, as much as it is through the spiritual pressure of God's grace. All we have to do is create a vacuum, to count ourselves as nothing — and immediately God fills the soul with His Power and Truth.

The paradox of apostolate is, then: the less we think we are, the more good we do. It was only when Peter had labored all night and taken nothing, that Our Lord filled his boat with the miraculous draught of fishes. The higher the building, the deeper the foundation; the greater the virtue, the more the humility.

God's instruments for good in the world are for that reason only the humble; reducing themselves to zero, they leave room for infinity, whereas those who think themselves infinite, God leaves with their little zero.

Even in the world, we find a natural basis for humility. As long as we are small, everything else seems big. A boy mounts a broomstick that is no more than four feet long and yet to him it is a Pegasus traveling through space; he can hear the hoofs beating the clouds as he clings to the "whistling mane of every wind." His world is peopled with giants because he is so little; tin soldiers to him are real soldiers fighting real battles, and the red of the carpet is the blood of the battlefield.

When he grows to be a big man, the giants shrink in size; the horses become broomsticks, and the soldiers are painted tin no more than three inches high. In the spiritual order, it is the same; as long as there is a God who is wiser than we, greater than we, more powerful than we, then the world is a house of wonders.

Truth is then something so vast that not even an eternity can sound its depths. Love then is so abiding that not even heaven can dull its ecstasies. Goodness becomes so profound that thanks must ever be on one's lips.

But just forget God, make yourself a god, and then your little learning is your title to omniscience. Then the saints become for you stupid fools; the martyrs, "fanatics"; the religious, "dumb"; confession, a "priestly invention"; the Eucharist, a "vestige of paganism"; heaven, a "childish fancy"; and truth, a "delusion." It must be wonderful to know so much, but it must be terrible to find out in the end that one really knows so little.

The second lesson to be derived from this Fourth Word from the Cross is that humility is truth. Humility is not an underestimation of our talents or gifts or powers, nor is it their exaggeration. A man who is six feet tall is not humble if he says he is only five feet four inches tall, just as he is not humble if he says he is seven feet tall. Humility is truth, or the recognition of gifts as gifts, faults as faults. Humility is dependence on God as pride is independence of Him.

It was that sense of independence or being without God which wrung out of the heart of Our Lord on the Cross this pitiable cry of abandonment: "My God, my God, why hast thou forsaken me?" The humble soul, conscious of his dependence on God, is always the thankful soul.

How many singers, orators, musicians, actors, doctors, professors ever think of thanking God for the special talents that made them outstanding in their profession? Out of the ten lepers who were made clean only one returned to give thanks. "Were not ten made clean? and where are the nine?" probably represents the proportion of the ungrateful who thank not because they are not humble.

The humble soul will always avoid praising his own good works and thus making void the virtue of his deeds. Self-praise devours merit; and those who have done good things to be seen by men, and who trumpet their philanthropies in the market places, will one day hear the saddest words of tongue or pen: "Thou hast already had thy reward."

The humble man, even though he be great in the eyes of the world, will esteem himself less than others, for he will always suspect that their internal greatness may far overreach his insignificant external greatness. He will therefore not flaunt his accidental superiority before his fellowman, for to do so is to prove one is not truly great. The really big men are the humble men; they are always approachable, kind, and understanding.

It is the little men who must put on airs. The really rich boy need not wear good clothes to impress his friends with his wealth, but the poor boy must do so to create the false impression of wealth. So it is with those who have nothing in their heads; they must be eternally creating the impression of how much they know, the books they have read, and the university from which they graduated.

The learned man never has to "seem" learned, as the saint never has to appear pious — but the hypocrite does. The fact that so many men take honors seriously, change their voices, and cultivate poses, proves they never should have had the honors — the honors were too big for them. They could not assimilate the honors; rather the honors assimilated them. Instead of wearing the purple, the purple wears them.

A sponge can absorb so much water and no more; a character can absorb so much praise and no more; the point of saturation is reached when the honor ceases to be a part of him and begins to stick out like a sore thumb. The truly great are like St. Philip Neri who one day, seeing a criminal being led off to prison, said: "There goes Philip Neri, except for the grace of God."

Suppose we began to be humble and esteemed others at least no less than ourselves.

Suppose to those who wounded us with their slanderous darts; we answered: "Father, forgive!" Suppose to those who classified us with thieves, we made the best of it and converted them saying: "This day, Paradise." Suppose out of those who shamed us before relatives, as Jesus was shamed before His Mother, we made a new friend for our heavenly Mother: "Behold thy son!" Suppose to those beneath us in worldly dignity we humbled ourselves and asked them for a drink: "I thirst!"

Suppose we began to be truthful and estimated ourselves at our real worth. If we did these things for but one hour, we would completely revolutionize the world. We are not wanting an example, for we have before our eyes Him who humbled Himself to the death on the Cross, who surrendered Divine consolation as Power put on the rags of weakness and Strength girded itself in abandonment, and, being God, appeared to be without God.

And why did He do this? Because we have been trying to lead our lives without God — to be independent. By choosing the humiliation of the Cross in reparation for pride, He takes us back again to the story of David and Goliath.

Goliath was a great giant clothed in an armor of steel and carrying in his hand a mighty sword. David was the shepherd boy without defensive steel and carrying no other weapon than a staff, and five little stones from a nearby brook. Goliath scorned him, saying: "Am I a dog, that thou comest to me with a staff?" David answered humbly, not trusting in his own power: "I come to thee in the name of the Lord ..." The outcome we know. The boy with a stone killed the giant with the armor and sword.

The victory of David symbolized the reality of Good Friday. Pride is Goliath. Our Lord is the humble David who comes to slay pride with the staff of His Cross and five little stones — five wounds, in hands, feet, and side. With no other weapon than these Five Wounds and the staff of the Cross do we gain victories over the Goliath of pride on the battlefield of our soul.

To the worldly they seem ill-fitted for battle, and impotent to conquer, but not if we understand God's plan from the beginning that:

" . . . the foolish things of the world hath God chosen that he may confound the wise; and the weak things of the world hath God chosen that he may confound the strong." It was with a cross and a crowned brow that God won the day. As Oscar Wilde puts it:

O smitten mouth! O forehead crowned with
thorn! O chalice of all common miseries!
Thou for our sakes that loved thee not has borne
An agony of endless centuries,
And we were vain and ignorant nor knew
That when we stabbed thy heart, it was our own
real hearts we slew.
Being ourselves the sowers and the seeds,
The night that covers and the lights that fade,
The spear that pierces and the side that bleeds,
The lips betraying and the life betrayed;
The deep hath calm: the moon hath rest: but we
Lords of the natural world are yet our own dread
enemy.

Nay, nay, we are but crucified, and though
The bloody sweat falls from our brows like rain,
Loosen the nails – we shall come down I know,

Stanch the red wounds – we shall be whole again,
No need have we of hyssop-laden rod,
That which is purely human, that is Godlike,
that is God.

Oscar Wilde

GLUTTONY

"I thirst."

GLUTTONY IS AN inordinate indulgence in food or drink, and may manifest itself either in taking more than is necessary, or in taking it at the wrong time, or in taking it too luxuriously. It is sinful because reason demands that food and drink be taken for the necessities and conveniences of nature, not for pleasure alone.

The Gospel describes Dives as being guilty of this sin. There is no mention in the story given to us by Our Blessed Lord that Dives was a wicked man. We have no record of him underpaying his servants or of being guilty of any moral turpitude. Our Lord tells us only that he was "clothed in purple and fine linen, and feasted sumptuously every day."

And there was a certain beggar named Lazarus, who lay at his gate full of sores, desiring to be filled with the crumbs that fell from the rich man's table, and no one did give him; moreover, the dogs came and licked his sores. And it came to pass that the beggar died and was carried by the angels into Abraham's bosom. And the rich man also died, and he was buried in hell. And lifting up his eyes when he was in torments, he saw Abraham afar off, and Lazarus in his bosom. And he cried and said: "Father Abraham, have mercy on me, and send Lazarus, that he may dip the tip of his finger in water, to cool my tongue; for I am tormented in this flame."

And Abraham said to him: "Son, remember that thou didst receive good things in thy lifetime, and likewise Lazarus evil things, but now he is comforted, and thou art tormented. And besides all this, between us and you, there is fixed a great chaos: so that they who would pass from hence to you, cannot, nor from thence come hither."

And he said: "Then, father, l beseech thee, that thou wouldst send him to my father's house, for I have five brethren, that he may testify unto them, lest they also come into this place of torments." And Abraham said to him,

"They have Moses and the prophets; let them hear them." But he said, "No, Father Abraham; but if one went to them from the dead, they will do penance." And he said to him, "If they hear not Moses and the prophets, neither will they believe, if one rise again from the dead."

If there is any indication of the present degeneration of society better than another, it is the excess of luxury in the modern world. When men begin to forget their souls, they begin to take great care of their bodies. There are more athletic clubs in the modern world than there are spiritual retreat houses; and who shall count the millions spent in beauty shops to glorify faces that will one day be the prey of worms.

It is not particularly difficult to find thousands who will spend two or three hours a day in exercising, but if you ask them to bend their knees to God in five minutes of prayer, they protest that it is too long. Added to this is the shocking amount that is yearly spent, not in the normal pleasure of drinking, but in its excess.

The scandal increases when one considers the necessary wants of the poor which could have been supplied by the amount spent for such dehumanization. The Divine judgment upon Dives is bound to be repeated upon many of our generation, who will find that the beggars for whose service they refused to interrupt their luxuries, will be seated at the Banquet of the King of Kings, while they, like Dives, will be the beggars for but a drop of water.

Some reparation had to be made for gluttony, drunkenness, and excessive luxury. That reparation began at the birth of Our Lord, when He who might have pulled down the heavens for His house-top and the stars for His chandeliers, chose to be rejected by men and driven as an outcast to a cave in the hillsides of the least of the cities of Israel.

The very first sermon He preached was a plea for detachment: "Blessed are the poor in spirit, for theirs is the kingdom of heaven." He began His public life by fasting forty days and bade men, "Be not solicitous for your life, what you shall eat, nor for your body, what you shall put on."

Traveling about as an itinerant prophet, He admitted He was as homeless as at His birth and that the beasts and birds had a better habitation than He: "The foxes have holes, and the birds of the air, nests; but the Son of Man hath not where to lay His head." There was no luxury in the way He dined, for we know of but one meal that He himself prepared, and it consisted only of bread and fish.

Finally, at the Cross, He is stripped of His garments and denied a death-bed, in order to go out of His own world as He came into it — Lord of it and yet possessing nothing. The waters of the sea were His and all the fountains of the earth had sprung up at His word; He it was who drew the bolt of Nature's waterfalls and shut up the seas with doors; He it was who said: "Whosoever drinketh of this water shall thirst again; but he that shall drink of the water that I will give him, shall not thirst for ever. If any man thirst, let him come to me, and drink."

But now He lets fall from His lips the shortest of the seven cries from the Cross and the one that expresses the keenest of all human sufferings in reparation for those who have had their fill: "I thirst."

A soldier immediately put a sponge full of vinegar on a stick and pressed it to His mouth. Thus was fulfilled the prophecy uttered by the Psalmist a thousand years before: "In my thirst, they gave me vinegar to drink."

He who fed the birds of the air is left unfed; He who changed water into wine now thirsts; the everlasting fountains are dry; the God-man is poverty-stricken. The Divine "Lazarus" stands at the door of the world and begs for a crumb and a drop, but the door of generosity is closed in His face.

Thus was reparation made for the luxury of eating and drinking. When Mirabeau was dying, he called for opium, saying, "You promised to spare me needless suffering . . . Support this head, the greatest head in France." When Christ is dying, He refuses the drug to alleviate His suffering. He deliberately wills to feel the most poignant of human wants, that He might balance in the scales of justice those who had more than they needed.

He even made Himself the least of all men by asking them for a drink — not a drink of earthly water. That is not what He wanted, but a drink for His thirsty heart — a drink of love: *I thirst for love.*

This word from the Cross reveals that there is a double hunger and a double thirst: one of the body, the other of the soul. On many previous occasions, Our Lord had distinguished between them: "Woe to you that are filled: for you shall hunger. Woe to you that now laugh: for you shall mourn and weep." "Blessed are ye that hunger now, for you shall be filled. Blessed are ye that weep now, for you shall laugh."

Then to the multitude who followed Him across the sea in search of bread, He said: "Labour not for the meat which perisheth, but for that which endureth unto life everlasting, which the Son of man will give you."

To the Samaritan woman who came to draw water at Jacob's well He foretold: "Whosoever drinketh of this water shall thirst again; but he that shall drink of the water that I will give him, shall not thirst forever: But the water that I will give him, shall become in him a fountain of water, springing up into life everlasting." But above all other references to the food and drink of the inner man as contrasted with that of the outer man, He promised the supreme nourishment of Himself: "For my flesh is meat indeed, and my blood is drink indeed."

It is in the light of this double hunger and thirst of body and soul that the distinction between dieting and fasting becomes clear. The Church fasts; the world diets. Materially there is no difference, for a person can lose twenty pounds one way as well as the other. But the difference is in the intention.

The Christian fasts not for the sake of the body, but for the sake of the soul; the pagan fasts not for the sake of the soul, but for the sake of the body. The Christian does not fast because he believes the body is wicked but in order to make it pliable in the hands of the soul, like a tool in the hands of a skilled workman.

That brings us down to the basic problem of life. Is the soul the tool of the body, or the body the tool of the soul? Should the soul do what the body wants, or should the body do what the soul wants? Each has its appetites, and each is imperious in the satisfaction of its wants. If we please one, we displease the other, and vice versa. Both of them cannot sit down together at the banquet of life.

The development of character depends on which hunger and thirst we cultivate. To diet or to fast — that is the problem. To lose a double chin in order to be more beautiful in the eyes of creatures or to lose it in order to keep the body tamed and ever obedient to the spiritual demands of the soul — that is the question. Human worth can be judged by human desires.

Tell me your hungers and your thirsts and I will tell you what you are. Do you hunger for money more than for mercy, for riches more than for virtue, and for power more than for service? Then you are selfish, pampered, and proud. Do you thirst for the Wine of Everlasting Life more than for pleasure, and for the poor more than for the favor of the rich, and for souls more than for the first places at table? Then you are a humble Christian.

The great pity is that so many have been so concerned with the body that they neglect the soul, and in neglecting the soul, they lose the appetite for the spiritual. Just as it is possible in the physiological order for a man to lose all appetite for food, so it is possible in the spiritual order to lose all desire for the supernatural. Gluttonous about the perishable, they become indifferent to the everlasting.

Like deaf ears, which are dead to the environment of harmony and blind eyes which are dead to the environment of beauty, so warped souls become dead to the environment of the Divine.

Darwin tells us in his autobiography that in his love for the biological he lost all the taste he once had for poetry and music, and he regretted the loss all the days of his life. Nothing so much dulls the capacity for the spiritual as excessive dedication to the material.

Excessive love of money destroys a sense of value; excessive love of the flesh kills the values of the spirit. Then comes a moment when everything seems to rebel against the higher law of our being. As the poet has put it, "All things betrayest thee, who betrayest me." Nature is so loyal to its Maker that it is always in the end disloyal to those who abuse it. "Traitorous trueness and loyal deceit" is its best poetic description, for in faithfulness to Him it will always be fickle with us.

The Fifth Word from the Cross is God's plea to the human heart to satisfy itself at the only satisfying fountains. God cannot compel men to thirst for the holy in place of the base, or for the divine rather than the secular. That is why His plea is merely an affirmation: "I thirst," meaning, "I thirst to be thirsted for." And His thirst is our salvation.

A twofold recommendation is hidden in this short sermon from the Cross: first, to mortify bodily hunger and thirst, and second, to cultivate a spiritual hunger and thirst.

We are to *mortify bodily hunger and thirst*, not because the flesh is wicked, but because the soul must ever exercise mastery over it, lest it become a tyrant. Quite apart from avoiding all excesses, the Cross commits us even to the minimizing of expenditures for luxuries, for the sake of the poor. How many ever think of foregoing an elaborate dinner and theater party, or a debut, out of genuine sympathy and affection for Christ's poor? Dives did not, and he lost his soul because of that forgetfulness. How many in less ample circumstances even mortify themselves one movie a month in order to drop its equivalent in the poor box, that He who sees in secret may reward in secret?

The Divine counsel concerning such restraint of bodily appetites is unmistakable. On one occasion, when Our Lord was invited to the home of the Prince of the Pharisees, He addressed the host himself saying: "When thou makest a dinner or a supper, call not thy friends, nor thy brethren, nor thy kinsmen, nor thy neighbors who are rich; lest perhaps they also invite thee again, and a recompense be made to thee. But when thou makest a feast, call the poor, the maimed, the lame, and the blind; And thou shalt be blessed, because they have not wherewith to make thee recompense; for recompense shall be made thee at the resurrection of the just."

The money we spend in the excesses of bodily hunger and thirst will do us no good on the last day; but the poor whom we have assisted by our restraint and mortification will stand up as so many advocates before the bar of Divine Justice, and will plead for mercy on our souls, even though they once were heavily laden with sin.

The Heavenly Judge cannot be bought with money, but He can be swayed by the poor. On that last day, the only one that really counts, will be fulfilled the beautifully prophetic words of the Mother of Our Lord: "He hath filled the hungry with good things, and the rich he hath sent empty away."

When such surrenders of the superfluous food and drink are made for the soul's sake, let it all be done in a spirit of joy. "And when you fast, be not as the hypocrites, sad. For they disfigure their faces, that they may appear unto men too fast. Amen, I say to you, they have received their reward. But thou, when thou fastest, anoint thy head and wash thy face; that thou appear not to men to fast, but to thy Father who is in secret; and thy Father who seeth in secret, will repay thee."

We are, in addition, to *cultivate a spiritual hunger and thirst.* Mortification of the bodily appetites is only a means, not an end. The end is union with God, the soul's desire. "Taste and see that the Lord is sweet." The great tragedy of life is not so much what men have suffered, but what they have missed. It comes within the compass of a few to satisfy their earthly desires with wealth, but there is no man living, who, if he willed it, could not enjoy the spiritual food and drink that God serves to all who ask.

And yet how few there are who ever think of nourishing their souls. How few there must have been in Jerusalem to have drawn from Our Lord the sweet complaint: "How often would I have gathered together thy children, as the hen doth gather her chickens under her wings, and thou wouldst not?"

Well indeed might the Saviour say to us, as we listen to the cry: "I thirst," the words he addressed to the woman at the well: "If thou didst know the gift of God, and who He is that saith to thee, Give me to drink; thou perhaps wouldst have asked of him, and he would have given thee living water."

But how many ask? Consider the greatest gift of God to men: the Bread of Life and the Wine that germinates virgins. How few avail themselves of the Divine presence to break their fast each morning on the Heavenly food of the soul!

How many are sufficiently conscious that Our Lord is present in the tabernacle, to pay a daily visit to Him in His Prison of Love? And if we do not, what does it witness to but the deadening of our spiritual sense. Our body would miss a dessert more than our soul would miss a Communion.

No wonder Our Crucified Redeemer thirsted for us on the Cross — thirsted for our unresponsive hearts and dulled souls. And let us not think that His thirst is a proof of His need, but of our own. He does not need us for His perfection any more than we need the flower that blooms outside our window for our perfection. In dry seasons we desire rain for the flower, not because we need the rain, but because the flower needs it.

In like manner, God thirsts for us, not because He needs us for His happiness, but because we need Him for our happiness. Without Him, it is impossible for us to develop. Just as certain diseases, such as rickets and anemia, arise in the body from a deficiency of necessary vitamins, so too our characters fail because of a deficiency of the Spirit.

The vast majority of men and women in the world today are so under-developed spiritually, that if a like deficiency showed in their bodies, they would be physical monstrosities.

How many millions of minds there are today that are devoid of one single satisfying truth that they can carry through life to sustain them in their sorrows and console them at their death? How many millions of wills there are that have not yet found the goal of life and which, because they are presently without it, flit like butterflies from one colored emotion to another, unable to find repose?

Let them cultivate a taste for something more than bread and circuses; let them sound the depths of their beings to discover there the arid wastes crying for the refreshment of everlasting fountains. Of course, these emaciated hungry souls are not altogether to blame. They have heard preachers without end preaching, "*Go to Christ!*" But what does that mean? Go back 1900 years? If so, then have they, not a right to doubt the Divinity of Him who could not project Himself through time?

Look up to heaven? If so, then what has become of His blessing, His forgiveness of sinners, His Truth that He said would endure unto the end of time? Where is His authority? His Power? His Life now? If it is not someplace on earth, then why did He come to earth? To leave only the echo of His words, the record of His deeds, and then to slip away leaving us only a history and its teachers?

Somewhere on earth today is His truth: "He that heareth you, heareth me." Somewhere on earth is His Power: "Behold, I have given you power . . ." Somewhere on earth is His Life: "The bread that I will give, is my flesh, for the life of the world." Where find it?

There is an institution on the face of the earth that claims to be that, and to those who have knocked at its portals and have asked for a drink has come the elixir of Divine Life and with it the peace that comes to those who drink and never thirst again, and eat and never hunger again.

To each and every one of us, inside and outside the Church, our Lord asks: "Will you accept the cup of My Love?" He took our cup of hate and bitterness in Gethsemane, and its dregs were so bitter that they made Him cry out: "My Father if it be possible, let this chalice pass from me."

But He drank every drop of it. If He drank our cup of hates why do we not drink His chalice of pardon? Why then, when He cries, "I thirst," do we reach Him vinegar and gall?

I cannot tell the half of it, yet hear
What rush of feeling still comes back to me,
From that proud torture hanging on His Cross,
From that gold rapture of His Heart in Mine.

I knew in blissful anguish what it means
To be a part of Christ, and feel as mine
The dark distresses of my brother limbs,
To feel it bodily and simply true,
To feel as mine the starving of His poor,
To feel as mine the shadow of curse on all,

Hard words, hard looks, and savage misery,
And struggling deaths, unpitied and unwept.
To feel rich brothers' sad satieties,
The weary manner of their lives and deaths,
That want in love, and lacking love lack all.
To feel the heavy sorrow of the world
Thicken and thicken on to future hell,
To mighty cities with their miles of streets,
Where men seek work for days and walk and
starve,
Freezing on river-banks on winter nights,
And come at last to cord or stream or steel.
The horror of the things our brothers bear!
It was but naught to that which after came,
The woe of things we make our brothers bear,
Our brothers and our sisters! In my heart
Christ's Heart seemed beating, and the world's
whole sin, —
Its crimson malice and grey negligence, —
Rose up and blackening hid the Face of God.

Arthur Shearly Cripps

SLOTH

"It is finished."

SLOTH IS A MALADY of the will that causes us to neglect our duties. Sloth may be physical or spiritual. It is physical when it shows itself in laziness, procrastination, idleness, softness, indifference, and nonchalance. It is spiritual when it shows itself in an indifference to character betterment, a distaste for the spiritual, a hurried crowding of devotions, lukewarmness, and failure to cultivate new virtue.

The classic description of the effects of sloth is to be found in the book of Proverbs: "I passed by the field of the slothful man, and by the vineyard of the foolish man: And behold, it was all filled with nettles, and thorns had covered the face thereof, and the stone wall was broken down. Which when I had seen, I laid it up in my heart, and by the example I received instruction. Thou wilt sleep a little, said I, thou wilt slumber a little, thou wilt fold thy hands a little to rest: And poverty shall come to thee as a runner and beggary as an armed man."

Of such indifference to duty Our Lord spoke in the Apocalypse: "But because thou art lukewarm, and neither cold nor hot, I will begin to vomit thee out of my mouth."

The Life and teaching of Our Lord lend no support to the slothful man. When yet only twelve years of age He speaks of being about His "Father's business" which was nothing less than redeeming the world. Then for eighteen years, He worked as a manual laborer transforming dead and useless things into the child's crib, the friend's table, Nazarene roofs, and the farmers' wagons, as symbols of His later work by which He would transform hard money changers and prostitutes into useful citizens of the Kingdom of Heaven.

Beginning a public life with calloused hands, He preached the Gospel of work: "I must work the works of Him that sent me, whilst it is day; the night cometh when no man can work." His whole life, in His own words, was spent not in receiving, but in giving: "the Son of man is not come to be ministered unto, but to minister, and to give his life as a redemption for many."

He earned the right to teach the necessity of work, and lest we live under any illusions that any other work is more important than the saving of souls, even the burial of our fathers, He said to the disciple who asked for such permission: "Follow me, and let the dead bury their dead."

To the young man who wished to be His disciple but first wanted to bid farewell to friends at home, Our Lord said: "No man putting his hand to the plough, and looking back, is fit for the kingdom of God." Laboring for bread alone is no fulfillment of His commandment, for to those who wanted more bread He pleaded, "Labor not for the meat which perisheth, but for that which endureth unto life everlasting, which the Son of man will give you."

The business of salvation is no easy task. There are two roads through this world and two gates into the future life. "Enter ye in at the narrow gate; for wide is the gate, and broad is the way, that leadeth to destruction, and many there are who go in there at. How narrow is the gate, and strait is the way that leadeth to life: and few there are that find it!"

Curiously enough, His invitation goes out only to those who labor for the eternal prize: "Come to me, all you who labor, and are burdened, and I will refresh you. Take up my yoke upon you, and learn of me, for I am meek and humble of heart: And you shall find rest to your souls. For my yoke is sweet, and my burden light."

So completely had He fulfilled the smallest detail of His Father's business that on the very night of His Agony, in the Upper Room in the presence of His Apostles, He could raise His eyes to heaven and pray: "Father . . . I have glorified thee on earth; I have finished the work which thou gavest me to do." Then the following afternoon, as the Carpenter is put to death by His own profession, He cries out from the Cross in a loud voice the final reparation for sloth and the song of triumph: "It is consummated."

He did not say, "I die," because death did not come to take Him. He walked to it to conquer it. The last drop in the chalice of redemption was drained; the last nail had been driven in the mansion of the Father's House; the last brush touched to the canvas of salvation! His work was done!

But ours is not. It is important to realize this for there are the slothful who justify themselves by saying they need only faith in Christ to save their souls. Surely He who worked so hard for the world's redemption, came not to dispense His followers from work. The servant is not above the master. Faith in Him alone does not save, for "faith without good works is dead." It is not enough for the student to have faith in his teacher's knowledge; he must also study. It is not enough for the sick to have faith in their doctor; their organism must cooperate with him and his medicine. It is not enough to believe that Washington was the "father of our country"; we must also assume and fulfill our duties as American citizens.

In like manner, it is not enough to believe in Christ; we must live Christ and, to some extent, die Christ-like. His words permit of no equivocation: "And he that taketh not up his cross, and followeth me, is not worthy of me. He that findeth his life shall lose it and he that shall lose his life for me, shall find it."

St. Paul understood the labor involved in being a Christian and wrote the same message to the Romans: "For if we have been planted together in the likeness of His death, we shall be also in the likeness of his resurrection." What He hath done with His human nature, we must do with ours — plant it in the soil of the Cross and await the Resurrection of the Eternal Easter.

Later on, to the Corinthians, Paul repeated it: "As you are partakers of the sufferings, so shall you be also of the consolation." And St. Peter, who knew well the scandal of the Cross pleaded for joy in reliving the Cross: "But if you partake of the sufferings of Christ, rejoice that when his glory shall be revealed, you may also be glad with exceeding joy."

There is no hope for the spiritually slothful in these injunctions. Our Lord is the die; we must be stamped by it. He is the pattern; we must be remodeled to it. The Cross is the condition; we must be nailed to it. Our Lord loved His Cross so much that He keeps its scars even in His glory. He who had won victory over death kept the record of its wounds.

If so precious to Him, they cannot be meaningless for us. In their preservation is the reminder that we too must be signed with those signs and sealed with those seals.

On Judgment Day, He will say to each of us: "Show Me your hands and feet. Where are your scars of victory? Have you fought no battles for truth? Have you won no wars for goodness? Have you made no enemy of evil?"

If we can prove we have been His warriors and show the scars on our apostolic hands, we shall enjoy the peace of victory. But woe unto us who come down from the Calvary of this earthly pilgrimage with hands unscarred and white!

Two lessons emerge from this Sixth Word from the Cross witnessing to His finished work and our own unfinished tasks: First, we must beware of spiritual sloth, for its penalties are tremendous; and second, we must work for a complete life.

The Gospel records three instances of sloth. There were the foolish virgins, chaste but lazy. The wise virgins fill their lamps with oil and wait to hear the step of the approaching bridegroom. The foolish virgins do not think of oil, and tired of waiting, they fall asleep. When the bridegroom comes, the wise virgins light their lamps and welcome the bridegroom. The foolish virgins go out to buy oil, but everybody is asleep, the shops are closed. They go back to the wedding feast, but the door is closed. They cry: "Lord, Lord, open to us." But His answer is: "Amen, I say to you, I know you not..." Our Lord concludes the parable with these words: "Watch, ye, therefore, because you know not the day nor the hour."

The second instance of sloth was the parable of the barren fig tree: "And the next day, when they came out from Bethania, he was hungry. And when he had seen afar off a fig tree having leaves, he came if perhaps he might find anything on it. And when he was come to it, he found nothing but leaves. For it was not the time for figs. And answering, he said to it: 'May no man hereafter eat fruit of thee any more forever."

The third was the parable of the buried talent. He who received five talents earned another five; he who had received two earned another two, but he who received one hid it in the ground. Of him, the lord of the servants said, "Wicked and slothful servant!. . Take ye away, therefore, the talent from him, and give it to him that hath ten talents. For to everyone that hath shall be given, and he shall abound: but from him, that hath not, that also which he seemeth to have shall be taken away. And the unprofitable servant cast ye out into the exterior darkness. There shall be weeping and gnashing of teeth."

Common to these three parables is the danger of sloth and the necessity of work. Purity without good works will not save us any more than it saved the foolish virgins. Those who do nothing run the risk of losing the little they have. In other words, it is possible to lose our souls by doing nothing. "How shall we escape if we neglect. .?" We lose our souls not only by the evil we do but also by the good we leave undone.

Neglect the body, and the muscles stiffen; neglect the mind, and imbecility comes; neglect the soul, and ruin follows. Just as physical life is the sum of the forces which resist death, so the spiritual life is to some extent the sum of the forces which resist evil. Neglect to take an antidote for a poison in the body, and we die by our neglect. Neglect to take precaution against sin, and we die the death merely because of neglect.

Heaven is a city on a hill. Hence, we cannot coast into it; we have to climb. Those who are too lazy to mount can miss its capture as well as the evil who refuse to seek it. Let no one think he can be totally indifferent to God in this life and suddenly develop a capacity for Him at the moment of death.

Where will the capacity for Heaven come from if we have neglected it on earth? A man cannot suddenly walk into a lecture room on higher mathematics and be thrilled by its equations if all during life he neglected to develop a taste for mathematics. A heaven of poets would be a hell to those who never learned to love poetry. And a heaven of Divine

Truth, Righteousness, and Justice would be a hell to those who never studiously cultivated those virtues here below. Heaven is only for those who work for heaven.

If we crush every inspiration of the Divine; if we drown every Godward inspiration of the soul; if we choke every inlet to Christ — where will be our relish for God on the last day? The very things we neglected will then be the very cause of our ruin. The very things that should have ministered to our growth will then turn against us and minister to our decay.

The sun, which warms the plant, can under other conditions also wither it. The rain, which nourishes the flower, can under other conditions rot it. The same sun shines upon mud that shines upon wax. It hardens the mud but softens the wax. The difference is not in the sun, but in that upon which it shines.

So it is with God. The Divine Life that shines upon a soul who loves Him softens it into everlasting life; that same Divine Life which shines upon the slothful soul, neglectful of God, hardens it into everlasting death.

Heaven and Hell are in like manner both effects of Divine Goodness. Their difference comes from our reaction to that goodness, and to that extent are also our creations. Both God and man are in different senses creators of heaven and hell.

A little heed then to this word from the Cross: "It is consummated." We finish our vocation as He finished His — on a cross and nowhere else. Only to the doers of the truth, and not to its preachers or its hearers, comes the reward of the crown. Doing implies the spending not of what we *have*, but of what we are.

We need have no undue fear for our health if we work hard for the Kingdom of God; God will take care of our health if we take care of His cause. In any case, it is better to burn out than to rust out.

Burning the candle at both ends for God's sake may be foolishness to the world, but it is a profitable Christian exercise — for so much better the light. Only one thing in life matters: Being found worthy of the Light of the World in the hour of His visitation.

"Take ye heed," He said. "Take ye heed, watch and pray. For ye know not when the time is. Even as a man who going into a far country, left his house, and gave authority to his servants over every work, and commanded the porter to watch. Watch ye, therefore (for you know not when the lord of the house cometh: at even, or at midnight, or at the cock crowing, or in the morning), lest coming on a sudden, he find you sleeping. And what I say to you, I say to all: Watch."

Not only must we beware of spiritual sloth, but we must also work for a completed life. The important word in the struggle against sloth is "finished." The world judges us by results; Our Lord judges us by the way we fulfill and finish our appointed tasks. A good life is not necessarily a successful life.

The sowers are not always the reapers. Those whom God destines only to sow receive their reward for just that, even though they never garnered a single sheaf into everlasting barns. In the parable of the talents, the reward is according to the development of potentialities and the completion of appointed duties.

One day Our Lord "sitting over against the treasury, beheld how the people cast money into the treasury and many that were rich cast in much. And there came a certain poor widow, and she cast in two mites, which make about half a cent. And calling his disciples together, he saith to them: Amen, I say to you, this poor widow hath cast in more than all they who have cast into the treasury. For all they did cast in of their abundance; but she of her want cast in all she had, *even* her whole living."

The result was trivial for the treasury, but it was infinite for her soul. She had not half done her duty, she had finished it. This is what is meant by completed living.

In the Christian order, it is not the important who are essential, nor those who do great things who are really great. A king is no nobler in the sight of God than a peasant. The head of government with millions of troops at his command is no more precious in the sight of God than a paralyzed child. The former has greater opportunities for evil, but like the widow in the Temple, if the child fulfills his task of resignation to the will of God more than the dictator fulfills his task of procuring social justice for the glory of God, then the child is greater. "God is no respecter of persons."

Men and women are only actors on the stage of life. Why should he who plays the part of the rich man glory in his gold and rich table and consider himself better than one who plays the role of the beggar begging a crumb from his table. When the curtain goes down, they are both men. So when God pulls down the curtain on the drama of the world's redemption, He will not ask what part we played, but only how well we played the role assigned to us. The Little Flower has said: that one could save one's soul by picking up pins out of love of God.

If we could create worlds and drop them into space from our fingertips, we would please God no more than by dropping a coin into a tin cup. It is not *what* is done, but *why* it is done that matters. A bootblack shining a pair of shoes inspired by a Divine motive is doing more good for this world than all the Godless conventions Moscow could ever convene.

It is the intention which makes the work. Duties in life are like marble, canvas, and stone. Marble becomes valuable because of the image given to it by the sculptor; canvas is ennobled by the picture of the artist, and stone is glorified by the pattern of the architect.

So it is with our works. The intention gives them value as the image gives the marble value. God is not interested in what we do with our hands, or our money, or our minds, or our mouths, but with our *wills*. It is not the work but the worker that counts.

Let those souls who think their work has no value recognize that by fulfilling their insignificant tasks out of a love of God, those tasks assume a supernatural worth. The aged who bear the taunts of the young, the sick crucified to their beds, the ignorant immigrant in the steel mill, the street cleaner and the garbage collector, the wardrobe mistress in the theater and the chorus girl who never had a line, the unemployed carpenter and the ash collector — all these will be enthroned above dictators, presidents, kings, and cardinals if a greater love of God inspires their humbler tasks than inspires those who play nobler roles with less love.

No work is finished until we do it for the honor and glory of God. "Whether you eat or drink, or whatever else you do, do all to the glory of God." When our lease on life runs out there are two questions will be asked. The world will ask: "How much did he leave?" The angels will ask: "How much did he bring with him?"

The soul can carry much, but in its journey to the judgment seat of God, it will be freighted down only with that kind of goods which a man can carry away from a shipwreck — his good works done for the glory of God. All that we leave behind is "unfinished." All that we take with us is "finished."

May we never die too soon! This does not mean not dying young; it means not dying with our appointed tasks undone. It is indeed a curious fact that no one ever thinks of Our Lord as dying too young! That is because He finished His Father's business. But no matter how old we are when we die, we always feel there is something more to be done.

Why do we feel that way, if it is not because we did not do well the tasks assigned to us. Our task may not be great; it may be only to add one stone to the Temple of God. But whatever it is, do each tiny little act in union with your Saviour, who died on the Cross, and you will *finish* your life. Then you will never die too young!

But if impatient, thou let slip thy cross,
Thou wilt not find it in this world again,
Nor in another; here, and here alone
Is given thee to suffer for God's sake.
In other words, we shall more perfectly
Serve Him and love Him, praise Him, work for
Him,
Grow near and nearer Him with all delight;
But then we shall not any more be called
To suffer, which is our appointment here,
Canst thou not suffer then one hour, — or two?

If He should call thee from thy cross to-day,
Saying, It is finished! – that hard cross of thine
From which thou prayest for deliverance,

Thinkest thou not some passion of regret
Would overcome thee? Thou wouldst say, "So
soon?

Let me go back and suffer yet awhile
More patiently; — I have not yet praised God."
And He might answer to thee, — "Never more.
All pain is done with." Whensoe'er it comes,
That summons that we look for, it will seem
Soon, yea too soon. Let us take heed in time
That God may now be glorified in us;
And while we suffer, let us set our souls
To suffer perfectly: since this alone,
The suffering, which is this world's special grace
May here be perfected and left behind. . . .

Endure, Endure, — be faithful to the end!

Harriet Eleanor Hamilton-King

COVETOUSNESS

"Father, into thy hands,
I commend my spirit."

COVETOUSNESS IS AN inordinate love of the things of this world. It becomes inordinate if one is not guided by a reasonable end, such as a suitable provision for one's family, or the future, or if one is too solicitous in amassing wealth, or too parsimonious in dispensing it.

The sin of covetousness includes therefore both the intention one has in acquiring the goods of this world and the manner of acquiring them. It is not the love of an excessive sum that makes it wrong, but an inordinate love of any sum.

Simply because a man has a great fortune, it does not follow that he is a covetous man. A child with a few pennies might possibly be more covetous. Material things are lawful and necessary to enable us to live according to our station in life, to mitigate suffering, to advance the Kingdom of God, and to save our souls.

It is the pursuit of wealth as an end instead of a means to the above ends, that makes a man covetous.

In this class of the covetous are to be placed the young woman who marries a divorced man for his money; the public official who accepts a bribe; the lawyer; the educator or clergyman who sponsors radical movements for Red gold; the capitalist who puts profits above human rights and needs, and the laborer who puts party power above the laborer's rights.

Covetousness is much more general in the world today than we suspect. It once was monopolized by the avaricious rich; now it is shared by the envious poor. Because a man has no money in his pockets is no proof that he is not covetous; he may be involuntarily poor with a passion for wealth far in excess of those who possess.

History bears witness to the fact that almost every radical economic revolutionist in history has been interested in only one thing: —

booty. The only poor people whoever attacked the rich and sought nothing for themselves were Our Lord and His followers, like St. Francis of Assisi.

There are very few disinterested lovers of the poor today; most of their so-called champions do not love the poor as much as they hate the rich. They hate all the rich, but they love only those poor who will help them attain their wicked ends.

Such covetousness is ruinous for man, principally because it hardens the heart. Man becomes like unto that which he loves, and if he loves gold, he becomes like it — cold, hard, and yellow. The more he acquires, the more he suffers at surrendering even the least of it, just as it hurts to have a single hair pulled out even though your head is full of them.

The more the sinfully rich man gets, the more he believes he is needy. He is always poor in his own eyes. The sense of the spiritual thus becomes so deadened, that its most precious treasures are bartered away for the trivial increases, as Judas sold his Master for thirty pieces of silver.

As St. Paul tells us, "The desire for money is the root of all evils, which some coveting have erred from the faith." *(1Timothy 6:10)* The Providence of God becomes less and less a reality, and if it still retains value, it is reduced to a secondary role; God is trusted as long as we have a good bank account.

When things go well we are quite willing to dispense with God, like the young man in the Gospel who came to our Lord only because he was being deprived of some of his father's estate. "Master, speak to my brother that he divide the inheritance with me." It was only when economic confusion arose that the young man had recourse to the Divine.

There are many in the world today who think that the only reason for the existence of the Church is to improve the economic order and if they do not have their fill, they assail the Church for failing. Well indeed might the Church answer in the words of Our Lord: "O man, who hath appointed me judge and divider over you?"

To turn man's heart away from perishable things to the eternal values of the soul, was one of the reasons for the Lord's visit to the earth. His teaching from the beginning was not only a warning against covetousness but a plea for a greater trust in Providence.

"Do not lay up for yourselves treasures upon the earth, where moth and rust consume, and where thieves break through and steal; but lay up for yourselves treasures in heaven, where neither moth nor rust consumes, and where thieves do not break through nor steal. For where thy treasure is, there will thy heart be also." *(Matthew 6:19-21)*

I say to you, therefore, do not be anxious about your life, what you shall eat or what you shall drink; nor about your body, what you shall wear. Is not the life of more consequence than the food, and the body than the clothing? Look at the birds of the sky, how they neither sow nor reap nor gather into barns, yet your heavenly Father feeds them! Are you not of much more value than they? Yet who among you by anxious thought is able to add a single span to his life?

And why should you worry about clothing? Observe the field-lilies, how they grow; they neither toil nor spin; yet I tell you that even Solomon in all his magnificence was not arrayed like one of them. But if God so clothes the grass of the field, which exists today and is thrown in the oven tomorrow, will He not much rather clothe you, O you of little faith?

"Do not, therefore, worry saying, "What shall we eat?" "What shall we drink?" or "What shall we wear?" for the heathen seek after all these things, and your heavenly Father knows that you need them all. But seek first the kingdom of God and His holiness, and all these things shall be given you besides. Do not then be anxious about tomorrow, for tomorrow will take care of itself. Quite enough for the day is it's own trouble." *(Matthew 6:25-34)*

The man who unduly loves riches is a fallen man, because of a bad exchange; he might have had heaven through his generosity, and he has only the earth. He could have kept his soul, but he sold it for material things. Camels will pass through eyes of needles more easily than the covetous will pass through the gates of heaven. It was easy of course to condemn the rich; our world is too full of those who are doing it now. But our economic revolutionists do it because they envy wealth, not because they love poverty.

It was not so with Our Divine Saviour. He Who condemned Dives and the man who ordered bigger barns the very day he died, and who thundered that no man could serve God and Mammon, lived His gospel. Not in a hospital, or a home, or a city, but in a stable in the fields did He bow entrance into the world He made. Not with money did He make money in the markets of exchange, but as a poor carpenter.

He earned His living with the two most primitive instruments used: wood and hammer. During His three years of preaching, not even a roof could He claim as His own: "The foxes have burrows, and the birds of the sky have nests, but the Son of Man has not a place where He may lay His head." *(Matthew 8:9,20)*

Then, at His death, He had no wealth to leave; His Mother He gave to John; His body to the tomb; His blood to the earth; His garments to His executioners. Absolutely dispossessed, He is still hated, to give the lie to those who say religion is hated because of its possessions.

Religion is hated because it is religion, and possessions are only the excuse and pretext for driving God from the earth. There was no quarreling about His will; there was no dispute about how His property would be divided; there was no lawsuit over the Lord of the Universe.

He had given up everything in reparation for covetousness, keeping only one thing for Himself that was not a thing — His Spirit. With a loud cry, so powerful that it freed His soul from His flesh and bore witness to the fact that He was giving up His life and not having it taken away, He said in farewell: "Father, into Thy Hands I commend My Spirit."

It rang out over the darkness and lost itself in the furthermost ends of the earth. The world has made all kinds of noise since to drown it out.

Men have busied themselves with nothing to shut out hearing it; but through the fog and darkness of cities, and the silence of the night, that awful cry rings within the hearing of everyone who does not force himself to forget, and as we listen to it we learn two lessons:

1. *The more ties we have to earth, the harder will it be for us to die.*

2. *We were never meant to be perfectly satisfied here below.*

In every friendship, hearts grow and entwine themselves together so that the two hearts seem to make only one heart with only a common thought. That is why separation is so painful; — it is not so much two hearts separating, but one heart being torn asunder.

When a man loves wealth inordinately, he and it grow together like a tree pushing itself in growth through the crevices of a rock. Death to such a man is a painful wrench, because of his close identification with the material. He has everything to live for, nothing to die for. He becomes at death the most destitute and despoiled beggar in the universe, for he has nothing he can take with him. He discovers too late that he did not belong to himself, but to things, for wealth is a pitiless master.

It would not allow him during life to think of anything else except increasing itself. Now he discovers too late that by consecrating himself to filling his barns, he was never free to save the only thing he could carry with him to eternity: — his soul. In order to acquire a part, he lost the whole; he won a fraction of the earth, now he will need only six feet of it.

Like a giant tied down by ten thousand ropes to ten thousand stakes, he is no longer free to think about anything else than what he must leave. That is why death is so hard for the covetous rich.

On the contrary, as the ties to earth become lessened, the easier is the separation. Where our treasure is, there is our heart also. If we have lived for God, then death is a liberation. Earth and its possessions are the cage that confines us and death is the opening of its door, enabling our soul to wing its way to its Beloved for which it had only lived and for which it only waited to die.

Our powers of dispossession are greater than our powers of possession; our hands could never contain all the gold in the world, but we can wash our hands of its desire. We cannot own the world, but we can disown it. That is why the soul with the vow of poverty is more satisfied than the richest covetous man in the world, for the latter has not yet all he wants, while the religious wants nothing; in a certain sense the religious has all and is perfectly happy.

It was such poverty of spirit raised to its sublimest peaks, which made the death of Our Lord so easy. He had no ties to earth. His treasure was with the Father, and His Soul followed the spiritual law of gravitation.

Gold, like dirt, falls; charity, like fire, rises: "Father, into Thy Hands I commend My Spirit."

The death of Our Lord on the Cross reveals that we are meant to be perpetually dissatisfied here below. If earth were meant to be a Paradise, then He who made it would never have taken leave of it on Good Friday. The commending of the Spirit to the Father was at the same time the refusal to commend it to earth. The completion or fulfillment of life is in heaven, not on earth.

Our Lord in His last Word is saying that nowhere else can we be satisfied except in God. It is absolutely impossible for us to be perfectly happy here below. Nothing proves this more than disappointment. One might almost say the essence of life is disappointment. We look forward to a position, to marriage, to ownership, to power, to popularity, to wealth, and when we attain them, we have to admit, if we are honest, that they never come up to our expectations.

As children we looked forward to Christmas; when it came, and we had our fill of sweets and tested every toy or rocked every doll, and then crept into our beds, we said in our own little heart of hearts: "Somehow or other, it did not quite come up to expectations." That experience is repeated a thousand times in life.

But why is there disappointment? Because when we look forward to a future ideal, we endow it with something of the infinity of the soul. I can imagine a house with ten thousand rooms studded with diamonds and emeralds, but I shall never see one. I can imagine a mountain of gold, but I shall never see one.

So with our earthly ideals. We color them with the qualities of our spiritual soul. But when they become realized, they are concrete, cabined, cribbed, confined. A tremendous disproportion thus arises between the ideal we conceived and the reality before us.

That disproportion between the infinite and the finite is the cause of disappointment. There is no escaping this fact. We have eternity in our heart, but time on our hands. The soul demands a heaven, and we get only an earth. Our eyes look up to the mountains, but they rest only on the plains. It is easier to strangle our ideals than it is to satisfy them. He who attains his earthly ideal smashes it.

To touch an ideal in this world is to destroy the ideal. "No man is a hero to his valet." We are no longer thirsty at the border of a well. The satisfaction of earthly ideals turns against us, like a cruel retort from one we paid an underhand compliment.

But there is no reason for being pessimists or cynics. Disappointment is no proof that there is no ideal, but only that it is not here. Just as we would have no eyes were there no beauties to see, and as we would have no ears were there no harmonies to hear, so we would have no appetite for the infinite were there no God to love.

In Him alone is the reconciliation of the chase and the capture. Here on this earth, we are buffeted between the two. The chase has its thrill for it is the pursuit of an ideal, the quest for satisfaction, and the march to victory. The capture to has its thrill for it is possession, enjoyment, and peace.

But while we live in time, we can never enjoy both together. The capture ends the excitement of the chase; and the chase without a capture is maddening, like having a refreshing spring withdrawn from our parched lips as we draw near to it.

How to combine the chase without the ennui of capture, and the capture without losing the joy of the chase? It is impossible here below, but not in heaven, for when we attain unto God, we capture the Infinite, and because He is Infinite, it will take an eternity of chase to discover the undiscoverable joys of Life, Truth, Love, and Beauty.

Such is the meaning behind the last and farewell word from the Cross. Centuries ago the sun shone upon plants and trees and imprisoned within them its light and heat. Today we dig up that light and heat in coal, and as its flames mount upward, we pay back our debt to the sun.

So now the Divine Light, that for thirty-three years has been imprisoning itself in human hearts, goes back again to the Father, to ever remind us that only by completing a similar circuit and commending our souls to the Father, do we find the answer to the riddle of life, and the end of disappointment and the beginning of eternal peace for our eternal hearts.

Everything is disappointing except the Redemptive Love of Our Lord. You can go on acquiring things, but you will be poor until your soul is filled with the love of Him Who died on the Cross for you. As the eye was made for seeing and the ear for hearing, so your spirit was made to be recommended back again to God.

If it had any other destiny the dying words of the Saviour would have betrayed that destiny. The spirit has a capacity for the infinite; the knowledge of one flower, the life of a single hour, the love of a minute do not exhaust its potencies. It wants the fullness of these things; in a word — it wants God.

The tragedy of our modern life is that so many put their pleasures in *desires* rather than in *discovery*. Having lost the one purpose of human living, namely God, they seek substitutes in the petty things of earth.

After repeated disappointments, they begin to put their happiness not in a pleasure, but in the *hunt* for it, in butterfly existences that never rest long enough at any one moment to know their inner desires; running races hoping they will never end; turning pages but never discovering the plot; knocking at doors of truth and then dashing away lest its portals be opened and they be invited in. Existence becomes a flight from peace, rather than an advance; a momentary escape from frustration instead of its sublimation in victory.

Every now and then there comes to some a light through the clouds of Calvary and the echo of the word commending a spirit to God, but instead of making a supreme effort to satisfy the goal of life, they crucify it.

"But the husbandmen said one to another, this is the heir; come, let us kill him, and the inheritance shall be ours. And laying hold of him, they killed him and cast him out of the vineyard."

Thus do some men believe that if they could drive God from the earth, the inheritance of sin would be there without remorse; and if they could but silence conscience, they could inherit peace without justice. It was just this mentality that sent Our Lord to the Cross. If the voice of God could be stifled, they believed they could enjoy the voice of Satan in peace.

Now take a different outlook on the world. How many, even of those who have killed conscience, can say: "l am happy; there is nothing I want"? But if you are not brave enough to say that, then why not seek? And why not seek in the one direction in which you know happiness lies?

At death, you will leave *everything*, but there is one thing you will not leave — your desire to life. You want the one thing the Cross brings you: — Life through death.

In its effulgence, the mystery of existence becomes clear. The Cross refers to *me*, personally and individually, as if no one else in the world ever existed. On the cross, He has traced for me in sacrifice, which is the sublimest of gestures, a program of life; submission to the Divine Will. He went down the dark road of Gethsemane to Calvary's death out of devotedness to God's glory and my salvation.

For my culpable self-indulgence, He atones by surrender of Himself. "He was wounded for our iniquities; He was bruised for our sins. The chastisement of our peace was upon Him." *(Isaiah 5:3-5)*.

If this Master of the world's symphony would miss my single note of virtue in the harmony of the universe; if this Captain of Wars would miss my spear in His battle for Goodness; if this Artist would miss my little daub of color in the masterpiece of redemption; if this Cosmic Architect would note the absence of my little stone in the building of His temple; if this Tree of Life would feel the fall of but my

little leaf to the sinfulness of earth; if this
Heavenly Father would miss me in the empty
chair at the banquet spread for the millions of
the children of God; if this Orator from the
Pulpit of the Cross would note my inattention
as I turned to glance at an executioner; if God
cares that much for me, then I must be worth
something since He loves me so!

But if Himself He come to thee, and stand
Beside thee, gazing down on thee with eyes
That smile, and suffer; that will smite thy heart,
With their own pity, to a passionate peace;
And reach to thee Himself and the Holy Cup
(With all its wreathen stems of passion-flowers
And quivering sparkles of the ruby stars),
Pallid and royal, saying 'Drink with Me;'
Wilt thou refuse? Nay, not for Paradise!
The pale brow will compel thee, the pure hands
Will minister unto thee; thou shalt take
Of that communion through the solemn depths.
Of the dark waters of thine agony,
With heart that praise Him, that yearns to Him

The closer through that hour. Hold fast His
hand, Though the nails pierce thine too! take
only care Lest one drop of the sacramental wine
Be spilled, of that which ever shall unite
Thee, soul and body to thy living Lord!

Harriet Eleanor Hamilton-King

THE SEVEN

VIRTUES

FULTON J. SHEEN

INTRODUCTION TO THE SEVEN VIRTUES

THESE MEDITATIONS on the Seven Last Words correlated to the seven virtues make no pretence to absoluteness. The Words are not necessarily related to the virtues but they do make convenient points of illustrations.

This book has only one aim: to awaken a love in the Passion of Our Lord and to incite the practice of virtue. If it does that in but one soul its publication has been justified.

THE FIRST VIRTUE

- Fortitude -

*"Father, forgive them, for they
know not what they do."*

THERE IS ENTIRELY too much psycho-
analysis in the world; what is needed is a little
more psycho-synthesis. Hearts and minds have
been analyzed to a point where they are nothing
more than a chaotic mass of unrelated nerve
impulses. There is need for someone to pull
them together, to give them a pattern of life and
above all, peace. The pattern around which we
shall psycho-synthesize all these soul-states
will be the Cross.

Here we are interested in three types of
souls: a) Those who suffer and mourn, saying
"What have I done to deserve this?"; b) those
who possess faith, but who through a love of the
world deny their faith or hide it; c) and those

who do not possess the faith, but are convinced of its truth and yet refuse to pay the price.

There is a virtue, which these three types of souls need for their peace, and that is the virtue of Fortitude.

Fortitude may be defined as that virtue, which enables us to face undismayed and fearlessly the difficulties, and dangers which stand in the way of duty and goodness. It stands midway between foolhardiness, which rushes into danger heedlessly, and cowardice, which flees from it recreantly. Because fortitude is related to bravery, it must not be thought that bravery is devoid of fear; rather it is control of fear. Fortitude is of two kinds, depending upon whether it is directed to a natural good or a supernatural good.

A soldier, for example, who braves the dangers of battle for love of country practices natural fortitude. But the saint who overcomes all difficulties and dangers for the sake of the glory of God and the salvation of his soul practices supernatural fortitude.

It is in the presence of the fear of death that Fortitude reaches its peak; that is why the highest peak of supernatural fortitude is martyrdom. We are here concerned only with supernatural fortitude.

This virtue reaches its peak in practice in the life of Our Divine Lord: He was primarily a Redeemer — God in the form of man saving men of whom He was King and Captain. "For God sent not his Son into the world, to judge the world, but that the world may be saved by him" (John 3:17).

His baptism was death, and He was "straitened until it be accomplished" (Luke 12:50). Being truly a man, He felt the fear every normal man feels in the face of danger. "If it be possible, let this chalice pass from Me" (Matthew 26:39); but resigned to the Father's business, He added: "Nevertheless not as I will, but as thou wilt" (Matthew 26:39).

No difficulty, however great, would deter Him from the Divine purpose of laying down His life for the redemption of many. Not even "twelve legions of Angels" (Matthew 26:53) would He permit to solace Him in His darkest hour, and not even a drug would He touch to His lips to deaden the pains of the Cross.

Solomon of old had said: "Give strong drink to them that are sad, and wine to them that are grieved in mind: Let them drink and forget their want, and remember their sorrow no more" (Proverbs 31:6,7).

The Talmud says it was the custom to put a grain of incense in the draft of those who were being led to death, to deaden the sense of pain.

This intoxicating draft, which was given Him as His hands and feet, were nailed to a tree of His own creation, He refused to drink (Matthew 27:34). He strides forth boldly to the high things of God. He will meet death in the full possession of His faculties — fearlessly.

But not in this was His fortitude greatest: when death is upon Him by His own submission, for "no man taketh it away from me: but I lay it down of myself" (John 10:18), His first word from the Cross is not in self-defense, not a protestation of His own innocence, not a fear of death nor a plea for deliverance, nor even fear of enemies.

Fear of death makes most men turn away from doing good. It makes even innocent men thoughtful of themselves as they proclaim their innocence to their executioners. Not so with Him. Fortitude reaches the peak of self-forgetfulness. On the Cross, He thinks only of others and their salvation.

For His first word is not about death, but about the good it will accomplish; it is directed not to His friends, His Apostles, or His believers who will proclaim His gospel, but to those who hate Him and His Apostles and His Church: "Father, forgive them, for they know not what they do" (Luke 23:34).

Often during His life, He preached: "Love your enemies: do good to them that hate you" (Matthew 5:44). Now that He is strong enough to ignore death, He the Conqueror bestows on His momentary conquerors the very thing they had forfeited by their sins — forgiveness.

Why is it that He appeals to His Father to forgive, and does not Himself forgive directly? Because He is looking at the crucifixion not from the human point of view, but from the Divine. They were wronging the Father by killing His Divine Son. The crucifixion is not murder; it is deicide.

Murder is a sin against God Who gave human life to human care. Deicide is a sin against God Who entrusted Divine Life to human love. It was not the candle of a man's life the executioners were snuffing out; it was the sun they were trying to extinguish.

The noon-day sun never darkened on murder, but it hid its face in shame as the Light of the World went into the momentary eclipse of death.

No stronger proclamation of His Divinity could have been uttered than for the Divine Son to ask the Divine Father to forgive the sons of men for their Golgothas, their swastikas, and their hammers and sickles. If He were only a man, He would have asked His own forgiveness, but being God, He asked His Father for the pardon of men.

Scripture does not record that anyone except the Thief on the right, within the hearing of that cry, repented or even regretted driving the nails and unfurling the flag of the Cross to the four winds of the world. There is not a single record that anyone else expressed a desire to follow Him or that they were touched by His calmness under fire.

Thus the world's greatest act of bravery when He who was thoughtless of self became thoughtful of others, went momentarily barren. They were apparently satisfied to sit and watch.

But it was for a bigger world than Calvary that He died, and for greater harvests than Jerusalem that He suffered. "And not for them only do I pray, but for them also who through their word shall believe in me" (John 17:20).

Now that the Divine Physician has prepared the medicine apply it to the first of our three types of souls, namely, those who suffer and mourn saying: "What have I done to deserve this?"

There are many good men and women tossing on beds of pain, their bodies wasted by long sickness, their hearts broken with woe and sorrow, or their minds tortured by the irreparable loss of friends and fortune. If these souls want peace, they must recognize that in this world there is no intrinsic connection between personal sin and suffering.

One day "Jesus passing by, saw a man, who was blind from his birth: And his disciples asked him: Rabbi, who hath sinned, this man, or his parents, that he should be born blind? Jesus answered: Neither hath this man sinned nor his parents" (John 9:1-3).

That brings us face to face with the inscrutable will of God which we cannot understand, any more than a mouse in a piano can understand why a musician disturbs him by playing. Our puny minds cannot understand the mysteries of God. But there are two basic truths, which such burdened souls, must never surrender. Otherwise, they will never find peace. First, God is love.

Hence anything He does to me deserves my gratitude, and I will say "thank you." God is still good even though He does not give me whatever I want in this world. He gives me only what I need for the next.

Parents do not give five-year-old boys guns to play with, though there is hardly a boy of five who does not want a gun. As Job put it: "If we have received good things at the hand of

God, why should we not receive evil?" (Job 2:10).

Second, the final reward for virtue comes not in this life, but in the next. As tapestries are woven not from the front but from the back, so too in this life we see only the underside of God's plan.

"My life is but a weaving
Between my God and me.
I may but choose the colors
He worketh skilfully.

Full oft He chooses sorrow,
And I, in foolish pride,
Forget He sees the upper,
And I the under, side."

Father Tabb

We are not to have our moods made by the world; the world should revolve about us; not us about the world. Like the earth in its revolution about the sun, we will carry our own atmosphere with us — resignation to the will of God. Then nothing can ever happen against our will because our will is the will of God.

This is not fatalism, which is subjection to blind necessity; it is patience, which is resignation to the will of the Divine Love who in the end can desire nothing but the eternal happiness and perfection of the one loved.

Fatalism is nonsense as the man walking precariously on the railing of a ship in a stormy sea proved when he said to the worried onlookers: "I'm a fatalist."

But patient resignation is exemplified by the child who said to her father: "Daddy, I do not know why you want me to go to the hospital for that operation. It hurts. I know only that you love me."

The shock of sorrow comes only to those who think this world is fixed and absolute, that there is nothing beyond. They think everything here below should be perfect. Hence they ask questions: "Why should I suffer? What have I done to deserve this?" Maybe you did nothing to deserve it. Certainly, Our Lord did nothing to deserve His Cross. But it came, and through it, He went to His glory.

The virtue to be cultivated then by such souls is what is known as Patience. Patience and Fortitude are related as the convex and concave sides of a saucer. Fortitude is exercised in the active struggle with dangers and difficulties, while Patience is the passive acceptance of what is hard to bear.

Our Lord on the Cross practiced Fortitude by freely and fearlessly meeting death to purchase our forgiveness; He practiced Patience by passively accepting the Father's will.

Being God, He could have stepped down from the Cross. Twelve legions of angels could have ministered to His wounds; the earth could have been His footstool, the seas as healing balm, the sun as His chariot, the planets His cortège, and the Cross His triumphal throne. But He willed to accept death to give us an example: "Not my will, but thine be done" (Luke 22:42).

Passive acceptance of God's will is Patience. Patience, other things being equal, is nobler than Fortitude; for in active works we may choose what pleases us and thereby sometimes deceive ourselves, but in resignation, to the crosses of life it is always God's will that we do.

"In your patience," He said, "you shall possess your souls" (Luke 21:19). In His Patience, He possesses His, for He did not choose His Cross, it was made for Him. He was fitted and patterned to it; we might almost say cut to fit it.

To take the Cross God sends us as He took the one given to Him, even though we do not deserve it, is the shortest way to identification with God's will which is the beginning of Power and Peace: Power because we are one with Him who can do all things; Peace because we are tranquil in the love of Him who is just.

Dare we call ourselves Christian and expect another road to heaven than that which Christ Himself traveled? Love leads the way — it is enough for us to follow the Beloved knowing that He loves and cares. Then instead of seeking to have a road free of obstacles to attain God, we shall, like hurdles in the race of life, make a race out of obstacles.

Embracing the crosses of life because given to us by Love on the Cross, does not mean that any of us ever reach the stage where our nature is willing to suffer. On the contrary, our nature rebels against it because it is contrary to nature. But we can will supernaturally what nature rejects, just as our reason can accept what the senses reject.

My eyes tell me I should not let the doctor lance the festering boil, for it will hurt. But my reason tells me that my senses must momentarily submit to the pain for the sake of a future good. So too we can will to bear the unavoidable ills of life for supernatural reasons. The First Word from the Cross suggests doing so for the sake of the remission of sins: "Forgive them."

In the business world, we contract debts and recognize our obligation and duty to acquit them. Why should we think that in the same moral universe we can sin with impunity? If then we bear the imprints of the Cross, instead of complaining against God let us occasionally think of offering them up to God for our own sins, or for the sins of our neighbors.

Of all the nonsense our modern world has invented, nothing surpasses the catchwords or claptrap we give the unfortunate or the sick: "Keep your chin up" or "Forget it." This is not solace, but a drug. Consolation is in explaining suffering, not forgetting it; in relating it to Love, not ignoring it; in making it an expiation for sin, not another sin. But who shall understand this unless he looks at a Cross and loves the Crucified?

The second type of soul who can be helped by this First Word from the Cross is he who, possessing the great gift of Faith, out of love of the world either hides it or denies it. This applies to those lukewarm Catholics who say: "Of course I ate meat at the party on Friday. Did you think I was going to have everyone laughing at me?" "Yes, I sent my son to a non-Catholic college. They are more social you know, and I don't want my boy to meet policemen's sons." Or, "When that chap at the office ridiculed the Mass, I did not say I was a Catholic, for the boss is anti-Catholic, and I might lose my job."

Doubtlessly such spineless Catholics would fit the spirit of the world better if they gave up their faith. Business men could then meet the challenge of chiseling competitors; the passion of youth could have its fling; husbands could have second wives; wives could have third husbands; both husbands and wives could find an alternative to self-restraint and thus escape the comparative poverty attendant upon raising a family; politicians could improve their chances for election if they were less Catholic; lawyers could be richer if they did not have to confess their sins and make amends; doctors could be wealthier if they were less conscientious and ceased to believe in Divine Justice.

There is no challenging the fact that Catholics could get on better with the world if they were less Catholic.

Not a single sentence can be found in the words of our Divine Lord promising you the love of the world because of your faith. But you can find a golden string of texts warning you that the world will hate you because you are His: "If you had been of the world, the world would love its own: but because you are not of the world, but I have chosen you out of the world, therefore the world hateth you" (John 15:19).

"Everyone therefore that shall confess me before men, I will also confess him before my Father who is in heaven. But he that shall deny me before men, I will also deny him before my Father who is in heaven . . . And he that taketh not up his cross, and followeth me, is not worthy of me. He that findeth his life shall lose it and he that shall lose his life for me, shall find it" (Matthew 10:32-33, 38-39).

"How narrow is the gate, and strait is the way that leadeth to life: and few there are that find it" (Matthew 7:14).

"For he that shall be ashamed of me, and of my words, in this adulterous and sinful generation: the Son of man also will be ashamed of him, when he shall come in the glory of his Father with the holy angels" (Mark 8:38; Cf. Luke 9:26).

"If we suffer, we shall also reign with him. If we deny him, he will also deny us" (2 Timothy 2:12).

"And if thy right hand scandalize thee, cut it off, and cast it from thee: for it is expedient for thee that one of thy members should perish, rather than that thy whole body go into hell" (Matthew 5:30).

The true followers of Christ were meant to be at odds with the world: The pure of heart will be laughed at by the Freudians; the meek will be scorned by the Marxists; the humble will be walked on by the go-getters; the liberal Sadducees will call them reactionaries; the reactionary Pharisees will call them liberals.

And Our Lord so warned: "Blessed are ye when they shall revile you, and persecute you, and speak all that is evil against you, untruly, for my sake: Be glad and rejoice for your reward is very great in heaven. For so they persecuted the prophets that were before you" (Matthew 5:11).

To all those compromising Catholics, a plea is made to practice the Fortitude of the Saviour on the Cross who, being thoughtless of death for the sake of our forgiveness, taught us to be thoughtless of the world's scorn for the sake of being forgiven.

We must not forget the word of Our Saviour: "He that shall deny me before men, I will also deny him before my Father who is in heaven" (Matthew 10:33). And if Catholics will not be strong in their love of Christ because of Christ, then let them be strong out of fear of the scandal of their weakness.

The example of a bad Catholic is most often appealed to as a justification for evil. Why is it that the world is more scandalized at a bad Catholic than a bad anything else if it be not because his fall is rightfully measured by the heights from which he has fallen.

And let this fortitude be not a muscular fortitude or abusive fortitude, but a fortitude brave enough to declare the belief in God even among the enemies who nail us to the cross of scorn, a fortitude like unto that of Eleazar, who, when commanded by Antiochus the enemy of the Jews to eat forbidden meat and who was advised by his own friends to do so, answered: "It doth not become our age . . . to dissemble . . . Though, for the present time, I should be delivered from the punishments of men, yet should I not escape the hand of the Almighty neither alive nor dead" (2 Maccabees 6:24, 26).

The third type of soul to whom this First Word offers Fortitude comprises those who are convinced of the truth of the faith but are unwilling to pay the price. A price does have to be paid for conversion, and that price is scorn. Many souls stand poised between an inner conviction that the Church is true and the certitude that if they embrace it, they must make enemies.

Once they cross its threshold a thinly veiled hostility often takes the place of friendship. They may be accused of having lost their reason; their jobs may be endangered; their friends who believed in freedom of conscience may now turn against them because their consciences acted freely; their love of liturgy will be scorned, as superstition and their supernatural faith will be called credulity.

If they joined a crazy cult or became a sun-worshipper or a Yogi follower or founded a new religion, their friends would say they acted within their constitutional rights; but when they join the Church, some will say they lost their minds, as they told Our Lord He had a devil.

Why this revolution of attitude once the threshold of the Church has been passed? Very simply because entering into the Church lifts us into another world — the supernatural world. It gives us a new set of values, a new objective, new ways of thinking, new standards of judgment, all of which are in opposition to the spirit of the world.

The world with its hatred of discipline, its courtesy to the flesh, and its indifference to truth cannot tolerate a life based upon the primacy of Christ and the salvation of souls. "I have chosen you out of the world, therefore the world hateth you. If you had been of the world, the world would love its own . . . [but] know ye, that it hath hated me before you" (John 15:19, 18).

Most people today want a religion which suits the way they live, rather than one which makes demands upon them. The result is that in order to make religion popular, too many prophets have watered down religion until it is hardly distinct from sentimental secularism.

Religion thus becomes a luxury like an opera, not a responsibility like life.

There is no doubt that a religion which makes concessions to human weakness will be popular; for example, one that denies hell for those who are unjust, and is silent about divorce for those who have repudiated their vows.

But as Catholics, we may not tamper with the message of Christ; for religion is of His making, not ours. Furthermore, the only religion which will help the world is one which contradicts the world.

Most Americans have been so disillusioned by a Cross-less Christ, that they are now looking back to the Cross as the only point of reference which gives meaning to life. They may not know how to phrase the conflict within, but they dimly perceive that all unhappiness is due to a conflict of wills: Family quarrels arise that way; misery of souls arises that way too when our selfish will contradicts the Divine will.

Peace, we are just discovering, is in the identity of our will with God who wills our perfection. When we disobey His will we are not asserting our independence; we are mutilating our personality as we might mutilate a razor by using it to cut a tree. Being made for God, we can be happy only with Him.

All our misery is traceable to that rebellion. All our peace is traceable to training the lower part of ourselves in service to Him. Hence the Cross, the symbol of that sacrifice inspired by love.

THE SECOND VIRTUE

- Hope -

"This day thou shalt be with me in paradise."

OUR CONCERN PRESENTLY is with two kinds of souls; the despairing and the presumptuous: either those who say, "I am too wicked for God to be interested in me," or those who say, "Oh, I need not worry about my sins. God will take good care of me in the end."

Both these statements are sins of exaggeration. The first is the sin of despair, which exaggerates Divine Justice; the second is the sin of presumption, which exaggerates Divine Mercy. Somewhere there is a golden mean where "Justice and mercy kiss" as the Psalmist puts it, and that is the virtue of Hope.

The virtue of Hope is quite different from the emotion of Hope. The emotion centers in the body and is a kind of dreamy desire that we can be saved without much effort. The virtue of

Hope, however, is centered in the will and may be defined as a divinely infused disposition of the will by which with sure confidence, thanks to the powerful help of Almighty God, we expect to pursue eternal happiness, using all the means necessary for attaining it.

The virtue of Hope lies not in the future of time, but beyond the tomb in eternity; its object is not the abundant life of earth, but the eternal love of God.

No stage was ever better set for the drama of Hope than Calvary. Seven centuries before, Isaias had prophesied that Our Divine Lord would be numbered with the wicked. In this hour the prophecy is fulfilled as two thieves, like unholy courtiers, stand unwilling guard on the King of Kings. Nothing could better reveal the contempt in which the Son of God was held than to have crucified Him between two common thieves.

To this ridicule of unholy companionship was added the mockery of a parade that passed before the throne of the central Cross. The Evangelists note them as they pass: rulers, soldiers, and passersby. "And the people stood beholding, and the rulers with them derided him, saying: He saved others; let him save himself if he be Christ, the elect of God" (Luke 23:35). "And the soldiers also mocked him, coming to him, and offering him vinegar" (Luke 23:36). "And they that passed by, blasphemed him, wagging their heads, and saying: Vah, thou that destroyest the temple of God, and in three days dost rebuild it; save thy own self; and if thou be the Son of God, come down from the cross" (Matthew 27:39-40).

As one gazes on that spectacle of three crosses silhouetted against a black and frightened sky, one sees in prospect the future judgment of the world; the Judge in the center and the two divisions of humanity on either side: The sheep and the goats; the blessed and the lost; those who love and those who hate; for the end shall be as the beginning, except that Christ shall appear for the final judgment not on the cross of ignominy but with the cross in glory in the clouds of heaven.

The spiritual development of the thief on the right, reveals how hope is born first out of fear, then out of faith. His conversion began the moment he feared. Like the thief on the left, he too had blasphemed that Man on the central Cross. Then suddenly turning his head he shouted across the face of Divine Mercy, to his blaspheming fellow thief: "Neither dost thou fear God, seeing thou art under the same condemnation? And we indeed justly, for we receive the due reward of our deeds; but this man hath done no evil" (Luke 23:40-41).

The fear of God of which this robber spoke was not a servile fear that God would punish them for their thefts; it was rather a filial fear based on reverence — a fear of displeasing Him who had done nothing to deserve such a humiliating death.

There is the first lesson: Hope begins with fear; hope involves fear because Hope is not certainty. We can, of course, be certain God will help us and give us sufficient strength to be saved, but we cannot be sure that we will always be faithful to His Grace.

God will not fail us; we need have no fear on that score. But we may fail God. The certitude that I am on the way to God does not exclude the fear that through some fault of mine, I may not come to His Blessed Presence.

Note the next step toward hope in the good thief as his fear led to faith, for "The fear of the Lord . . . is wisdom" (Job 28:28).

In a single moment, a soul with a genuine fear of God can come to a greater understanding of the purpose of life than in a lifetime spent in the study of the ephemeral philosophies of men. That is why death-bed conversions may be sincere conversions. The hardened soul disbelieves in God until that awful moment when he has no one to deceive but himself. Once the spark of salutary fear of God had jumped into the soul of the thief from the flaming furnace of that central Cross, fear gave way to faith. His next words were believing.

No longer was Christ an innocent man, nor an exiled upstart, nor a mock monarch. He was a King! Those thorns were His crown; that Cross was His throne; He had Omnipotent Power; that nail was His scepter; He was a Saviour — that is why He forgave His enemies.

Out from the full heart of the thief, there welled up the hopeful petition: "Remember me when thou shalt come into thy kingdom" (Luke 23:42). He could not desire what he did not know; he could not hope in what he did not believe. The thief had faith in the Son of God; now he could hope.

And that hope born of fear and faith received its immediate response: "This day thou shalt be with me in paradise" (Luke 23:43).

Above the blasphemous, raucous background of others shouting "Himself He cannot save," he heard: "This Day." He had only asked for the future, but the answer was more than he had hoped: "This Day." His arms were still pinioned, but he felt them loosen at the sound of "This Day"; his body was still racked by pain, but he felt it freshen at "This Day." His life was of little value — but his soul took on eternal worth as he heard "This Day . . . Paradise." A thief had learned to call "Lord" to One whom he despised. And the Lord can forgive sins . . . Such is the beginning of Hope.

Two thieves there were: One who loved and one who hated. Each was on a cross. Neither the good nor the bad ever escape the cross. One thief was saved; therefore, let no one despair. One thief was lost; therefore, let no one presume.

The two extremes to be avoided then are presumption and despair. Presumption is an excess of hope, and despair is a defect of hope. Presumption is an inordinate trust in Divine Mercy, a hope of pardon without repentance, a heaven without merit.

A word to the presumptuous who hope for a death-bed conversion to make their peace with God, and who say: "God would not send me to hell," or "I have lived a fairly decent life, so I have nothing to worry about," or "I know I am a sinner, but no worse than my neighbor; why should I worry? God is merciful."

When you make the statement "God is good," what do you mean? Only this: "God is insensible to evil. He is good because He is unmindful of my wickedness." You forget that God is good precisely because He is the enemy of evil. A healthy man is not indifferent to disease; nor is a government good because it ignores crimes and injustice. Why then should you think that God will be complacent about that which you refuse to accept in others?

If you really believed that God is good, would you not be scrupulous about offending Him? Do you not do that much for your friends? The nobler a person is, the more you dread offending him. Even for those whom you do not love, you show respect.

Will you then exploit Divine Goodness and deceive One in whom you repose the confidence of salvation? Will you forget that Goodness wounded by cynicism avenges itself?

If you lose your earthly friends by prostituting their generosity, will you not in like manner lose your Heavenly Friend by presuming? Will you make Divine Mercy the excuse for greater sinning? ls, there not in every life a last pardon as there is also a last sin? Have we not allotted to each of us a final sin, which fills up the "bag of sin" and seals our eternity?

You may sin a thousand times and be forgiven, but like the man who threw himself into a river a hundred times, each time to be rescued by the bridge-tender, you may be told by the rescuer: "Someday you will throw yourself into the river, and I may not be here to pull you out."

What we all have to realize is that when we sin we turn our back on God. He does not turn His back on us. If we are ever to see His face again we must turn around, that is, turn from sin. That is what is meant by conversion. "Turn ye to me, saith the Lord of hosts" (Zechariah 1:3).

God cannot save us without that conversion; if we die in our unrepentant sin, we are forever turned away from God. Where the tree falleth there it lies. There is no reversal of values after death.

We cannot love sin during life and begin to love virtue at death. The joys of heaven are the continuance of the Christ-like joys of earth. We do not develop a new set of loves with our last breath. We shall reap in eternity only what we sowed on earth. If we loved sin, we shall reap corruption; but we shall never gather grapes from thistles.

The Justice of God is not separable from His Goodness. If He were not Just, He would not be Good. Because He is Goodness, His Justice pardons; because He is Justice, His Goodness expiates. The thief on the right saw the need of Justice the moment he admitted, "We suffer justly"; that is why immediately he felt the response of Goodness: "This Day . . . Paradise."

Then let not our presuming moderns who pile sin on sin think that they can insult God until their lease on life has run out and then expect an eternal lease on one of the Father's mansions. Did He who went to Heaven by a Cross intend that you should go there by sinning?

Let us consider the other type of soul: the despairing. As presumption forgets Divine Justice, so despair forgets Divine Mercy. Modern despair is not only hopeless about eternal life, which it doubts but even about earthly life, which it mocks. Never before in the history of Christianity has despair been so abysmal. Today there is everywhere an anticipation of catastrophe, an appalling sense of unpredictability and impending disaster.

In the past, men recovered from despair either by returning to the glories of the past or by looking forward to a crown beyond the cross; but now that minds have lost faith in God, they have only this world to give them hope.

Since that has turned against them, they feel a conscious rupture with hope. They curse a meaningless existence, succumb to a continuous exasperation with uncertainty, and yield to a suicidal intent to escape the inescapable.

There are two causes for modern despair: Sensuality and sadness. It is a fact that those poets who have most ridiculed the future life and those writers who have poured the most scorn on sin and Divine Justice were themselves most abandoned to sensuality.

The singers of voluptuousness are always the singers of despair. This is because sensuality produces continuous disillusionment. Its pleasures must be repeated because of their unsatisfyingness; therefore, they make hungry where most they satisfy.

Being deceived so many times by the alluring promises of the flesh, its addicts feel that all life is a deceit. Having been fooled by that which promised pleasure, they conclude that nothing can give pleasure. The fruit of pessimism blossom on the tree of a dissolute life.

From another point of view, sensuality begets despair because by its very nature it is directed to a sensual object, and an excessive dedication to the carnal kills the capacity for the spiritual. Delicate hands lose their skill by handling rough stones, and souls lose their appetite for the Divine by undue attachment to the flesh. The eyes that refuse to look upon the light soon lose their power to see: "Having eyes, [they] see . . . not" (Mark 8:18).

Hope implies love; but if love is centered in the corporal, the soul is deadened to all that is not carnal: It finds less and less satisfaction in duty, family, work, profession, and, above all else, God. There is time only for the wicked joy to which one is slave.

Naturally, the future life and heaven and the Cross cease to move such a person. There is no desire except the biological; the future begins to be disgusting. From a stage where there is no time for God, they reach another where there is no taste for God. Thus does a world, which forgot love for sex, pay its terrible penalty in the despair, which calls life meaningless because it has made its own life a wreck.

The second cause of despair is sadness. Sadness does not mean sorrow caused by a death, but rather a surrender to states of depression because of a consciousness of sin and unworthiness. Many falls produce melancholy; repeated defeats induce despair.

St. Paul speaks of carnal excesses and greed for money as the feeble compensations for the one who experiences melancholy induced by multiplied sin: "Who despairing have given themselves up to lasciviousness, unto the working of all uncleanness unto covetousness" (Ephesians 4:19).

Despair, born of the loss of God, also ends in persecution. In their impiety, such souls would kill the God they left. That is why wherever you find an atheistic government in the world today, you find "purges." Not being able to tolerate their own inner sadness, they must compensate for it by killing hope in others.

Each despairing soul must decide for itself the reason for despair. Regardless however of how multiplied or grievous your sins may have been, there is still room for hope. Did not Our Lord say: "For I came not to call the just, but sinners" (Mark 2:17); and on another occasion "there shall be joy in heaven upon one sinner that doth penance, more than upon ninety-nine just who need not penance" (Luke 15:7).

If He forgave the thief, and Magdalene, and Peter, why not you? What makes many in old age sad is not that their joys are gone, but that their hopes are gone. Your earthly hopes may decrease with the years, but not heavenly hope. Regardless of the sinful burden of the years, God's mercy is greater than your faults.

Only when God ceases to be infinitely merciful and only when you begin to be infinitely evil, will there be reason for despair; and that will be never; Peter denied Our Lord, but Our Lord did not deny Peter. The thief cursed Christ, but He did not curse the thief. If we had never sinned, we could never call Christ Saviour.

The Divine Invitation has never been annulled: "Come to me, all you that labour, and are burdened, and I will refresh you" (Matthew 11:28). That invitation is not only for the weary; it is also for the sinful.

If you insist that you are disgusted with yourself, remember that you can come to God even by a succession of disgusts. What does your disgust mean except that everything earthly has failed you? That is one of the ways God makes you feel hunger for the Divine. Do you not crave food most when you are hungry? Do you not want water most when you are thirsty?

Your own disgust, if you knew it, is the distant call of Divine Mercy. If then the poverty of your merits makes you shrink from the Divine Presence, then let your needs draw you to Him.

The principal reason for the increase of nervous disorders in the world is due to hidden guilt or unatoned sin locked on the inside until it festered. These souls are running off to psychoanalysts to have their sins explained away when what they need is to get down on their knees and right themselves with God.

When disgusted with our sins we can go into a confessional box, become our own accuser, hear the words of absolution Our Lord Himself gave, make amends and start life all over again, for none of us want our sins explained away; we want them forgiven. That is the miracle of the Sacrament of Penance and the rekindling of Hope.

"If I had sat at supper with the Lord
And laid my head upon that saving breast
I might have turned and fled among the rest –
I might have been that one who left the board
To add the high priests' silver to his hoard.
Had our Redeemer stooped to wash my feet,
Would I have washed my neighbor's clean and sweet
Or thrice denied the Christ I had adored?

"Long have I grieved that I was not St. Paul
Who rode those seas and saw the tempest toss
The ships he sailed in when he heard the call
To preach the risen Christ and gain through loss.
Tonight I envy most among them all
That thief who hung repentant on his cross."

Alexander Harvey

THE THIRD VIRTUE

- Prudence -

"Behold thy son; behold thy mother."

THE GREATEST CRISIS in the history of the world was the arrest and conviction of a Man found guilty of no other charge than an excess of love. What was tragic about that crisis reaching from a Garden to a Cross was: Man failed!

Peter, James, and John, who had been given the flashing light of the Transfiguration to prepare them for the dark night of Olives, slept as His enemies attacked. Judas, who had heard the Divine admonition to lay up treasures in Heaven, peddled his Master for thirty pieces of silver — for Divinity is always sold out of all proportion to due worth.

Peter who had been made the Rock and Key-bearer, warmed himself by a fire and with an atavistic throwback to his fisherman days, cursed and swore to a maidservant that he knew not the man.

As Pilate submitted to the crowd the choice of Christ or a revolutionary upstart, the mob chose Barabbas. Finally, on Calvary where were the men? Where were those whom He cured? Peter was not there, nor his brother Andrew, nor James, nor any of the other Apostles except John, who might not have been there had it not been for the encouragement given him by Mary.

But though men failed in this crisis, there is no instance of a single woman failing. In the four trials, the voice heard in His defense was that of a woman, Claudia Procul, the wife of Pontius Pilate, warning her husband not to do anything unjust to that just man. Events proved that the politician was wrong and the woman right.

On the way to Calvary, it is the woman who offers consolation, first Veronica wiping away the blood and sweat from His Sacred Face to receive the reward of Its imprint on her towel; then the holy women to whom the Prisoner turned suggesting that only such multiplied mercies and charities as their own could avert catastrophe for their children.

Again on Calvary, it is woman who is fearless, for there are several of them at the foot of the Cross. Magdalene, among them as usual, is prostrate. But there is one whose courage and devotion was so remarkable that the Evangelist who was there indicated the detail that she was "standing." That woman was the Mother of the Man on the Central Cross.

When we realize that He who is pinioned to that Cross is the Son of God and therefore possessed of Infinite Wisdom and Power, we are at first inclined to wonder why she should not have been spared the sorrow of Golgotha.

Since He had made her of incomparable beauty of body and soul, why should He not keep those eyes made for Paradise from gazing on a Cross? Why not shield ears attuned to the Divine Word from the blasphemies of ungrateful humans? Since preserved from original sin, why should its penalties be visited upon her? Must Mothers go to gallows with their sons? Must the innocent eat the bitter fruit planted by the sinful?

These are questions of false human wisdom, But God's ways are not our ways. Our Blessed Lord willed her presence there. Since He was the second Adam undoing the sin of the first, Mary would be the new Eve proclaiming the glory of womanhood in the new race of the redeemed.

The woman Eve would not be so cured that her most glorious daughter could not undo her evil. As a woman had shared in the fall of man, so woman should share in his redemption. In no better way could Our Lord reveal woman's role in the new order than by giving John, that disciple whom He loved above the others, to His Mother whom He loved above all: "Son! Behold thy Mother . . . Woman! Behold thy son! "

The Kingdom of God was born! Heavenly prudence had chosen the right means to reveal the new ties born of redemption. Mary was to be our Mother, and we her children.

The Saviour's death was at the same time a birth; the end of a chapter of crucifixion was the beginning of the chapter of a new creation.

As light is instantaneous in dispelling darkness so the Divine Saviour wills that not even a moment shall intervene between breaking down the attachments to Satan by sin and the incorporation of man into the Kingdom of God. She exchanges her Son for the advantages of the Passion and receives its first fruit — John. He had kept His word: "l will not leave you orphans" (John 14:18).

On the Cross was Wisdom Incarnate, dying that we might live. If Our Saviour could have thought of any better means of leading us back to Him, He would have put us in other hands than hers.

There are many falsehoods told about the Catholic Church: One of them is that Catholics adore Mary. This is absolutely untrue. Mary is a creature, human, not Divine. Catholics do not adore Mary. That would be idolatry. But they do reverence her.

And to those Christians who have forgotten Mary, may we ask if it is proper for them to forget her whom He remembered on the Cross? Will they bear no love for that woman through the portals of whose flesh, as the Gate of Heaven, He came to earth?

One of the reasons why so many Christians have lost a belief in the Divinity of Christ is because they lost all affection for her upon whose white body, as a Tower of Ivory, that Infant climbed "to kiss upon her lips a mystic rose."

There is not a Christian in all the world who reverences Mary who does not acknowledge Jesus her Son to be in Truth the Son of the Living God. The prudent Christ on the Cross knew the prudent way to preserve belief in His Divinity, for who better than a Mother knows her son?

The gift of Mary did something to man, for it gave him an ideal love. To fully appreciate this fact, dwell for a moment on the difference between two faculties: The intellect, which knows, and the will, which loves.

The intellect always whittles down the object to suit itself. That is why the intellect insists on examples, explanations, and analogies. Every teacher must accommodate himself to the mentality of his class, and if the problem, which he is presenting, is abstract and complicated, he must break it up into the concrete, as Our Lord described the mysteries of the Kingdom of God in parables.

But the will never works that way. While the intellect pulls down the object of knowledge to its level, the will always goes out to meet the object.

If you love something, you lift yourself up to its level; if you love music you subject yourself to its demands, and if you love mathematics you meet its conditions. We tend to become like that which we love. Boys who love gangsters are already the making of gangsters. As our loves are, that we are. We scale mountains if the object loved is on a mountain; we jump down into the abyss if the object loved is there.

It follows that the higher our loves and ideals, the nobler will be our character. The problem of character training is fundamentally the inculcation of proper ideals. That is why every nation holds up its national heroes, that citizens may become like to them in their patriotism and devotion to country.

If we have heroes and ideal prototypes for those who love sports, the stage, country, army, and navy, why should there not be an ideal in the all-important business of leading a good life and saving our souls?

That is precisely one of the roles the Blessed Mother of our Divine Lord plays in Christian life: An object of love so pure, so holy, and so motherly that to be worthy of it we refrain from doing anything which might offend her.

There has hardly ever been a mother in the history of the world who did not at one time or another say to her son or daughter: "Never do anything of which your mother would be ashamed." But what these mothers say is only an echo from the Cross, when Our Divine Lord gave us His Mother as our mother. In giving her to us, He was equivalently saying: "Never do anything of which your Heavenly Mother would be ashamed."

The nobler the love, the nobler the character, and what nobler love could be given to men than the woman whom the Saviour of the world chose as His own Mother?

Why is it that the world has confessed its inability to inculcate virtue in the young? Very simply because it has not co-related morality to any love nobler than self-love. Things keep their proportion and fulfill their proper role only when integrated into a larger whole.

Most lives are like doors without hinges, or sleeves without coats, or bows without violins; that is, unrelated to wholes or purposes which give them meaning.

If, for example, a speaker concentrates upon his hands, wonders whether he should put them in his pockets or behind his back, it will not be long until he feels he is all hands.

The modern emphasis on sex is a result of tearing a function away from a purpose, a part away from a whole. It can never be handled properly unless integrated to a larger pattern and made to serve it.

That is, to some extent, the role Our Blessed Mother plays in the moral life of our Catholic youth. She is that ideal love for which lesser and baser loves and impulses are sacrificed. Just as a skilled orator so integrates his hands into the pattern of speech that he is never conscious of their presence, so the

Catholic youth maintains that healthy self-restraint out of respect for one whom he loves.

The level of any civilization is the level of its womanhood. What they are, men will be, for, to repeat, love always goes out to meet the demands of the object loved. Given a woman like the Mother of Our Lord as our supernatural Mother, you have one of the greatest inspirations for nobler living this world has ever known.

In this hour as never before the world needs to hear again this third word from the Cross. It needs the inspiration of the Good Woman. Unfortunately, the woman who is admired today is not the virtuous woman, but the beautiful woman — and by beautiful is meant not that inner beauty of the king's daughter, but that beauty which is only skin deep and sometimes only powder deep.

Glance at the advertisements flashed across the pages and billboards of our country! They are for the most part pictures of women who ten years from now would not be accepted for the same advertisement because they will have lost what they now possess — a passing beauty.

Our modern world does not really love woman; it loves only her external beauty. If it loved woman, it would love woman as long as she is woman. But because it loves the mask of a woman, it ignores the woman when the mask disappears.

The alarming increase of divorces in our land and the consequent break-up of family life is due principally to the loss of love for the ideal in womanhood. Marriage has become identified with pleasure, not with love. Once the pleasure ceases, love ceases. The woman is loved not for what she is in herself but for what she is to others. The tragedy of such a state is not only what it does for woman, but also what it does for man.

How restore love for woman as woman? By giving as the object of life's love a woman who has given Life and Love to the world — a Woman who is beautiful on the outside all the days of her life, because she is beautiful on the inside. That was the means Our Lord chose on the Cross to remake the world: Remake man by remaking the woman.

Conceived in the Divine Mind, sculptured by the creative fingers of the Heavenly Sculptor, touched by ever radiant color from the palette of heaven, the Artist on the Cross points to His masterpiece and says to man: "Behold the Woman!"

There is told a legend which illustrates the intercessory power of Our Blessed Lady: It seems that one day Our Blessed Lord was walking through the Kingdom of Heaven and saw some souls who had got in very easily. Approaching Peter at the Golden Gate, He said: "Peter, I have given to you the keys to the Kingdom of Heaven. You must use your power wisely and discreetly. Tell Me, Peter, how did these souls gain entry into My Kingdom?" To which Peter answered: "Don't blame me, Lord. Every time I close the door, Your Mother opens a window."

When amidst the thousand and one allurements of this world you know not which way to turn, pray to the Woman — the Virgin most prudent. She knows the true from the false, for in the language of Joyce Kilmer:

At the foot of the Cross on Calvary
Three soldiers sat and diced
And one of them was the devil
And he won the Robe of Christ.

I saw him through a thousand veils
And has not this sufficed?
Now, must I look on the devil robed
In the radiant robe of Christ?

He comes, his face is sad and mild
With thorns, his head is crowned
There are great bleeding wounds in His feet
And in each hand a wound.

How can I tell, who am a fool
If this be Christ or no?
Those bleeding hands outstretched to me
Those eyes that love me so!

I see the robe – I look, I hope
I fear – but there is one
Who will direct my troubled mind.
Christ's Mother knows her Son.

O Mother of Good Counsel, lend
Intelligence to me
Encompass me with wisdom
Thou Tower of Ivory!

"This is the man of lies" she says
"Disguised with fearful art:
He has the wounded hands and feet
But not the wounded heart."

Beside the Cross on Calvary
She watched them as they diced
She saw the devil join the game
And win the Robe of Christ.

"The Robe of Christ"
MAIN STREET AND OTHER POEMS
*by **Joyce Kilmer***
©1917 Doubleday, Doran & Company Inc.

THE FOURTH VIRTUE

- Faith -

"My God! My God!
Why hast thou forsaken me?"

HOW MANY WHO profess no formal religion could tell what they disbelieve? The question is put that way because years ago many who did not have faith knew what they disbelieved and why; today those who do not have faith do not even know what they disbelieve. Having abandoned all certitudes, they have no standards by which to judge even their own agnosticism.

And now, with the depression, war, and its consequent insecurity, they have begun to doubt their own doubts. The words 'progress' 'evolution' and 'science' which once thrilled them and gave them the illusion of faith, now leave them cold.

Many today feel that their life is discontinuous; that each act of their will is unrelated to any other; that their bad actions of the past, like a spent arrow, are gone and forgotten; that their life because ephemeral is unrelated to any responsibility, and that their last week's self is no longer their worry, nor what they will be next week their moral concern.

Their life is like a Japanese lantern, made up of thousands of designs, but without unity. They may know much, but they cannot put their fields of learning into a unity.

Their knowledge is like the shelves in a drug store, filled with bottles of wisdom one unrelated to another, but not like a living thing in which organs, cells, and functions flow into a unity of purpose.

What they need to do is put a candle inside the Japanese lantern of their life: or a soul into their discontinuous chemical existence in order to recover the meaning of life, and that candle and that soul is faith.

Faith is not, as too many believe, an emotional trust; it is not a belief that something will happen to you; it is not even a will to believe despite difficulties. Rather faith is the acceptance of a truth on the authority of God revealing. It, therefore, presupposes reason. What credit is to business that faith is to religion.

Before extending you credit, the businessman must have a reason for extending that credit, namely, your ability to pay debts and your honesty. So it is with faith. You cannot start religion with faith, for to believe someone without a reason for belief is credulity and superstition.

The principal cause for the decline of religion in America is the irrational and groundless character of belief. Unless the foundation is solid the superstructure soon totters and falls. Try out the experiment and ask those who call themselves Christians why they believe and the majority of them will be found unable to give a reason.

When anyone asks us to join the Church, he is not immediately accepted. He must first undergo instructions of between forty and one hundred hours extending over several months.

Converts are not first told: "You must believe everything the Catholic Church teaches" but rather "You must have a reason for believing its teachings." Absolutely nothing is taken for granted. We do not say: "We will start with God." No! We start with the world. Using reason we, first prove the existence of God and His nature.

Enquiry precedes conviction. Enquiry is a matter for reason which weighs the evidence and says: "I ought to believe." But submission is an act of the will. It is at this point many fail, either because too absorbed by the pleasures of the world, or because fearful of the scorn of others.

But once it is admitted, thanks to the illumining grace of God, that Christ is the Son of God; there can be no picking and choosing among the parts of His Gospel.

Since Truth is life, it must like a living babe, be accepted in its entirety. Just as we are not falsely broadminded about life and accept a child on condition he has no arms or only one eye, so neither can we say we will believe Christ when He talks about lilies of the field and not believe Him when He talks about the sanctity of the family. It is all or nothing. "He that gathereth not . . . scattereth" (Matthew 12:30).

That is why the condition of becoming a Catholic is the total, complete and absolute submission to the authority of Christ and its prolongation in the Church. A Catholic may be defined as one who made the startling discovery that God knows more than he does.

Faith is related to reason as a telescope to the eye, which does not destroy vision, but opens new worlds hitherto closed to it. We have the same eyes at night as we have in the day, but we cannot see at night because we lack normally the additional light of the sun.

Let two minds with exactly the same education, one without and the other with faith, look on a piece of unleavened bread in a monstrance. The one sees bread; the other adores the Eucharistic Lord. One sees more than the other because he has a light which the other lacks — the light of faith.

For some illustrations of the virtue of faith, we look in particular to the Fourth Word spoken from the pulpit of the Cross.

For almost three hours Our Lord hung upon the Cross, while the sun wore the crêpe of darkness in mourning for the Light of the World. Men might look on the sad spectacle of a Crucified Lord, but the sun could not endure it and hid its face.

The Evangelists record the Fourth Word as being spoken when darkness covered the earth, which means that it was as night, not only in nature but in the heart and soul of Jesus. It was a moment of mysterious voluntary surrender of Divine consolation, a second of seeming God-forsakenness.

Man had already abandoned Him. They chose Barabbas to Him; they even begrudged Him enough of their earth to stretch out and die as they lifted Him above it on a tree.

Now God seems to abandon Him, as in the midst of the stygian blackness at high noon He spoke this time in Hebrew, the language of the Prophet and the Psalm. The tones were loud and clear: "Eli, Eli, lamma sabacthani" — "My God, my God, why hast thou forsaken me?" (Matthew 27:46).

During His life some of His disciples left Him and walked with Him no more; only the night before at the Last Supper He said: "Behold, the hour cometh, and it is now come, that you shall be scattered every man to his own, and shall leave me alone . . ." (John 16:32).

That hour was upon Him now. He refused to be spared what His adopted brethren must share. He was "made sin" for us by taking upon Himself the condition which sin merited. What did sin merit? Abandonment by God.

Creatures turned against the Creator; the sheep rebelled against the Shepherd, the pilgrims left the fountains of living waters and dug for themselves broken cisterns that could hold no water. He willed to experience that isolation and abandonment. Hence the words: "Why hast thou forsaken me?"

And yet it was not total abandonment for it was prefaced by God: "My God, my God!" The sun does not abandon its task to light a world because temporarily overshadowed by a cloud. Because these misty shapes hide its light and heat, we still know a day of dawning is near.

Furthermore, the Fourth Word was a verse from a Psalm of faith which ends: "He hath not slighted nor despised the supplication of the poor man. Neither hath he turned away his face from me: and when I cried to him, he heard me" (Psalm 21:25).

In the perspective of this Word of Faith there are these three practical conclusions:

1) The object of faith is God, not the things of earth. Too many interpret faith as that which should release us from the ills of earth and assume that if we do suffer it is because we lack faith. This is quite untrue. Faith in God is no assurance that we will be spared the "arrows of outrageous fortune."

He was not. Why should we? It was His enemies who thought that if He were one with God, He should not suffer, for when He said: "Eli, Eli" they, imagining He called for Elias, sneered: "See whether Elias will come to deliver him" (Matthew 27:49). Because He was not delivered, they concluded He must be wicked. No! Faith does not mean being taken down from a cross; it means be lifted up to heaven — sometimes by a cross.

The only times some people think of God is when they are in trouble, or when their pocketbook is empty, or they have a chance to make it a little fatter. They flatter themselves that at such moments they have faith when really they have only earthly hope for good luck.

It cannot be repeated too often: faith bears on the soul and its salvation in God, not on the baubles of earth.

2) Scripture states that when they crucified Christ, darkness covered the earth. That is exactly the description of our modern world. If the darkness of despair, the black-outs of peace make our world wander blindly, it is because we have crucified the Light of the World.

Witness within the last twenty years how religion has been nailed to the Cross in Russia, scourged in Germany, crowned with thorns in Spain, martyred in Poland, and lashed in Mexico.

No wonder our statesmen know not which way to turn: they are either putting out or permitting to be put out the only Light which illumines the pathways of justice and peace.

It may be that our woes are the last stage of sin. For a century or more governments and people have abandoned God; now God is abandoning them. It is a terrible punishment when a just God strikes, but it is more terrible when He does not but leaves us alone to our own devices to work out the full consequences of our sins.

We are at the end of a tradition and a civilization which believes we could preserve Christianity without Christ: religion without a creed, meditation without sacrifice, family life without moral responsibility, sex without purity, and economics without ethics.

We have completed our experiment of living without God and have proven the fallacy of a system of education which calls itself progressive because it finds new excuses for sins.

Our so-called progressiveness did we but realize it, is like unto the progressive putrefaction of a corpse. The soul is gone, and what we call change is only decay.

There is no stopping it except by reversing the process by which we drove God out of the world, namely by relighting the lamp of faith in the souls of men.

3) Here is a common burden of all believers in God. There is, unfortunately, a far greater unity among the enemies of God than among His friends. On the one hand, we have the spectacle of Hitler and Stalin burying their mutual hatreds because they found a greater hatred — God and religion.

On the other hand, what are we believers in God doing to preserve religion, morality, and culture? Too often we wage a civil war, attacking one another, while a common enemy storms our altars. This does not mean we must abandon creeds, and water down the milk of religion to a point where it would no longer nourish.

The Catholic Church for one would never do that because since its truths are God-made, they cannot be man-unmade. We are trustees not creators of faith.

But we do recognize that with Protestants and Jews we have God, morality, and religion in common. In the name of God, let us, Jews, Protestants and Catholics, do two things: 1)

Realize that an attack upon one is an attack upon all since we are all one in God; it is not Tolerance we need, but Charity; not forbearance but love.

3) Begin doing something about religion and the least we can do is to say our prayers: to implore God's blessings upon the world and our country; to thank Him for His blessings, and to become illumined in the fullness of His truth. There is entirely too much talk about religion and not enough action.

If we followed the same rules for health that we do about religion, we would all be bedridden. It is not enough to talk about the necessity of health; we must do something practical about it, for example, eat, exercise and rest.

So it is with religion. We must nourish ourselves with the truths of God, exercise our spiritual muscles in prayer, mortify ourselves of those things which are harmful to the soul, and be just as scrupulous in avoiding moral evil as we are in avoiding physical evil.

Faith being a virtue is a habit, — not an acquired habit like swimming, but an infused habit given to us by God in Baptism. Being a habit, it grows by practice.

The ideal is to reach a point in practice, where, like unto Our Lord on the Cross, we witness to God even amidst abandonment and the agony of a crucifixion.

THE FIFTH VIRTUE

- Temperance -

"I Thirst."

THERE IS A WORLD of difference between what we need and what we want. We need those things which are essential for a normal, comfortable human existence; but we want more than that. Our needs are quickly satisfied, but our wants rarely.

The day our Blessed Lord multiplied the loaves and fishes the Evangelist records that each person had his fill and was satisfied. But just suppose that Our Lord instead of giving food which they needed, miraculously multiplied money and gave each of them the equivalent of a ten-dollar bill. How many, do you think, would have been satisfied with one bill? Money is a want; food is a need.

Because our needs are limited, but our wants are unlimited, a virtue is necessary to

restrain our inordinate appetites and desires —
and that virtue is called temperance. It has for
its object the regulation of the sensible
appetites by reason.

The two strongest appetites in man are
eating and drinking which sustain his
individual life and the sexual act which
propagates his social nature. Excesses in these
appetites are the sources of the two sins of
gluttony and lust. Temperance is the virtue
which moderates them for the sake of the soul.

Temperance must not be confused either
with Puritanism, which because of the abuse of
a thing would take away its use; or with license,
which would interpret all restraint as an
infringement of liberty. Rather, there is a
golden mean, as revealed in Our Lord's first
miracle at Cana, where He changed water into
wine to satisfy the individual appetite and
blessed the married couple for the satisfaction
of the creative instinct.

There is no consolation here for those
gloomy souls who would kill the joy of living,
nor for those frivolous souls who would isolate

pleasure from the end of living, namely, the salvation of the soul.

Temperance reaches its peak in Him who came to preach the hard way of the cross and yet began it by serving wine and assisting at a marriage feast. For that reason, the extremists who want all fast or all feast were never pleased with His Temperance.

As He said to them on one occasion: "For John came neither eating nor drinking; and they say: He hath a devil. The Son of man came eating and drinking, and they say: Behold a man that is a glutton and a wine drinker a friend of publicans and sinners" (Matthew 11:18-19). It is so hard to please those who are looking for faults.

Finally, on the Cross, He gave us His Fifth Word — the revelation of the philosophy of temperance. Racked by the burning fever of crucifixion, like a dying soldier on a battlefield His lips craved for water. There was a physical foundation of the cry: "I thirst" (John 19:28).

But it looked to something else. St. John who was at the foot of the Cross records that He said it "that the scriptures might be fulfilled" (John 19:28).

A thousand years before the Psalmist had prophesied that hour: "And they gave me gall for my food, and in my thirst, they gave me vinegar to drink" (Psalm 68:22).

The cry was not a cry of weakness, nor selfishness, but a proclamation that the material exists for the spiritual; the appetites and thirsts of earth must be the stepping stones to the hunger and thirst for the kingdom of God and His Justice.

From this Word we learn two lessons of Temperance: First, the material exists for the spiritual. Christ expressed a physical thirst for a spiritual reason, namely, the fulfillment of prophecy as a proof of His divinity. In like manner, every material thing on the face of this earth, from salt to flesh, must be for us, a means, not an end — a bridge, not a goal of life.

A glutton does not respect this order; he does not eat to live but lives to eat. He subordinates life to one of its conditions. The glutton or the drunkard is really a person without a sense of humor. He takes food and drink too seriously; he always misses the reference.

He takes drink so seriously that he forgets it was meant to assist locomotion, not to impede it; he takes flesh so seriously that he forgets it was meant to solder life, not to scorch it.

Why are there so many unhappy marriages today? Because instead of marrying for the reason that human love is the vestibule to the Divine, they marry wondering how long they will be married. On the way back from the Justice of the Peace they are already preparing for divorce as one says to the other: "I will love you for two years and six months."

There was once a time when a man who married a woman would no more have thought of divorcing her than of murdering her. But those were the days when men loved because they believed in God; now they lust because they believe in Freud — for if this world is all there is, then why not get all you can and by whatever means you can.

It is only in the Church today that "life without lust is born," because she teaches that the use of flesh conditions salvation. But in our modern divorce-mad world "lust without life shall die."

Because temperance teaches us that the earthly exists for the heavenly, the motive of a Christian is far different from the motive of a pagan.

Take two persons who by cutting down on their food lose twenty pounds each. Materially, twenty pounds off a pagan is the same as twenty pounds off a Christian. But the motive in each case is quite different. The pagan diets; the Christian fasts. The pagan diets for the sake of his bodily appearance; the Christian fasts for the sake of his soul. Each received his corresponding reward, either the praise of men who love leanness or the praise of God who loves virtue.

The tragedy of so much dieting, from a Catholic point of view, is how much restraint, or shall we say fat, that goes to waste. That is why one of the first questions in our Catechism is: "Of which should we take more care, our soul or our body?" And the answer is: "We should take more care of our soul, for 'what doth it profit a man if he gain the whole world, and suffer the loss of his immortal soul?'"

It is the rigid adherence to this principle that the material exists for the spiritual, which makes the Catholic school one of the greatest training grounds for character in the world. Little children are taught as soon as they enter school to 'give up' certain things during Lent — not because candy is bad, but in order that they might be self-controlled and self-possessed. It is the contrary to the pagan philosophy of 'self-expression' or doing whatever you please.

A boiler that refuses to keep within the limits and blows up is self-expressive. A drunkard is self-expressive or liquor-possessed because he is not self-possessed. Liquor is not his servant; he is its slave. We Catholics do not eat meat on Friday because we love our Lord. That is the day on which He died, and out of loving memory for this redemption we give up the pleasure of meat — and most of us Catholics hate fish — because He gave up His life for us. Is that anything to be scorned?

The basis of the Catholic secret of temperance and discipline is exchange. All life is founded on exchange: "What exchange shall a man give?" We get light in exchange for heat; bread in exchange for a dime. If you want to be an expert in mathematics you have to give up being an expert in tennis; if you want to give your body all its satisfactions, you have to give up the joys of the soul. We have to pay for everything.

Every joy demands that another be left untouched. Every step forward requires an austerity, but that is not because there are no rewards on the other side of the hill, but only because we cannot see what is on the other side of the hill.

We must choose then between God and Mammon; flesh and spirit. "No man can serve two masters." If we want to save our soul for eternity, we must discipline our body in time. And we do this not with sadness but with gladness, after the example of Him "who having joy set before him endured the Cross."

A saint is always joyful, but our modern pleasure-hunter is always melancholy. He is not really happy because he laughs too much. His laughter is artificially stimulated from the outside by a stooge with a wise-crack; it is not a joy that proceeds from the inside because of a duty fulfilled out of love of God. Happiness comes from self-possession through temperance, not from self-expression through license.

The second lesson of temperance in this Fifth Word is given us by the soldier who shared his wine with Our Lord. The cry of Our Lord was not addressed to anyone in particular, but as others wondered what to do, he did it. Scripture says "he ran."

There was no irresoluteness about his service; only one thought dominated his mind: "His need is greater than mine." The Gospel notes that he filled the sponge. It was unusual for an executioner to share rations with the one to be executed, but there was something very un-criminal about that man on the central cross.

The wine he gave was not much, but God considers not the gift of the giver, but the love of the giver. The soldier could not reach the lips of Our Lord, so he placed the sponge on a reed and touched it to the lips of the Saviour. He had shared his wine with his Creator, and if he knew it, also with his Saviour. And until the crack of doom, his act like that of Magdalene shall be recorded among men.

As he restrained himself in the use of his lawful possessions out of love of the suffering, so must we share our treasures out of love for the poor. Here again, the motive of sharing is more important than the deed. The reward we will get for our giving depends on the intention of our giving.

We love those who love us — but there is no great reward in this, for "do not the heathens this." But we must love even our enemies that we may be children of Our Father who is in heaven. Loving enemies out of a divine intention is worth more than loving friends out of a personal satisfaction.

The philanthropists who give millions to erect art museums, libraries, and playgrounds out of purely humanitarian reasons, will not further their eternal salvation as much as the poor widow who gives a nickel to a poor man on the street because in his need she sees the poverty of Christ. It is simply a matter of bookkeeping.

Suppose you wanted to establish a credit for purchases. Naturally, if you deposited your money on credit in a furniture store, you could not expect it to be honored at an automobile factory. In like manner, if you give lavishly to be credited by mankind, you cannot expect to be credited by Christ for eternal salvation. Millions given to perpetuate a family name will avail the soul nothing at the moment of judgment.

This does not mean that money given for art institutes and playgrounds do not avail for eternal salvation, but that they avail only on condition they were given for that motive, that is, in His name: "For whosoever shall give you to drink a cup of water in my name, because you belong to Christ: Amen I say to you, he shall not love his reward" (Mark 9:40).

St. Paul, emphasizing that charity or the love of God alone makes deeds profitable unto salvation, is even more emphatic: "If I should distribute all my goods to feed the poor, and if I should deliver my body to be burned, and have not charity, it profiteth me nothing" (1 Corinthians 13:3).

There is a story told of a woman who gave a fortune motivated by human glory, and very occasionally a meager gift for a spiritual intention. When she went to heaven St. Peter showed her a tiny insignificant little house, which was dwarfed by all the mansions surrounding it. "I cannot live in that," said the woman. St. Peter answered: "Sorry, lady. That was the best I could do with the materials you sent me."

It is one of the paradoxes of Christianity that the only things that are really our own when we die is what we gave away in His name. What we leave in our wills is snatched from us by death; but what we give away is recorded by God to our eternal credit, for only our works follow us. It is not what is given that profits unto salvation; it is why it is given.

That is why a friendly meal given to an enemy in the name of Him Who loved us when we were His enemies, is worth more on the day of our judgment than a ten-million-dollar hospital given to perpetuate a family name.

There is no injustice in this. Each gets the reward he wanted: In one instance, the love of Christ; in the other the memory of men. Of the latter, Our Lord said the saddest words ever spoken: "They already have their reward."

For those who wish to cultivate the virtue of temperance and to be self-possessed, these two specific recommendations are made: First, each day practice at least three trivial mortifications, for example, giving up the ninth cigarette, holding back the sarcastic word, returning a kindly answer to a sneer, or sealing the lips on the scandal you just heard, which probably, like all scandals, is 99 44/100 percent untrue.

Second, the magnitude of the mortification is not as important as the love of God for which it is done. Great sacrifices without love are worthless for the soul; nor because they are great does it follow they were done with love; it is the motive that matters — do them out of love of God.

Then amid the crosses and trials of life, you may catch their relation to the Cross, which alone gives a pattern to the contradiction of life.

May we all, like unto the soldier, Joyce Kilmer, as he trudged across the fields of France, see in every aching shoulder, feverish brow, and burning hand, the vision of Christ with His Cross:

My shoulders ache beneath my pack
(Lie easier, Cross, upon His back).

I march with feet that burn and smart
(Tread, Holy Feet, upon my heart).

Men shout at me who may not speak
(They scourged Thy back and smote Thy cheek).

I may not lift a hand to clear
My eyes of salty drops that sear.

(Then shall my fickle soul forget
Thy Agony of Bloody Sweat?)

My rifle hand is stiff and numb
(From Thy pierced palm red rivers come).

Lord, Thou didst suffer more for me
Than all the hosts of land and sea.

So let me render back again
This millionth of Thy gifts.   Amen.

POEMS, ESSAYS AND LETTERS
*by **Joyce Kilmer***
©*1914, 1918 Doubleday, Doran & Company Inc.*

THE SIXTH VIRTUE

- Justice -

"It is consummated."

CALVARY IS NOT A HISTORY everyone likes to hear recalled, and generally, those who most shrink from the sight of the Saviour on the Cross are the very ones who delight in the grotesque murder stories in our tabloids and follow with bold interest the harrowing details of a sex crime.

Why is it that the lover of horror cannot stand the sight of the crucifix? Why is it that the fanatics of murder stories are so cold to the story of the world's greatest sacrifice? The answer is that unlike all other crimes the crucifix is self-accusing.

We can look on other scenes of injustice without feeling we are involved in them; but we cannot look on a crucifix without feeling that we had something to do with it, either for better or worse; either as a robber brought before his victim for judgment, or as a drowning man brought before his rescuer for thanks.

In the face of all things else, we can remain somewhat indifferent, for inhuman injustice the issues of right and wrong are not always clear-cut. But on Calvary there is an absoluteness; there are no streaks of grey, no blurred edges, only a straight collision of black and white, of good and evil — and there is no 'No Man's Land' between them.

It is the epitome of the struggle of the world; we are involved in it to the extent that we are involved in the conflict of good and evil. It would be convenient at times if we could wash our hands of the whole affair as Pilate tried to do; but deeper than the blood on Lady Macbeth's hands, not all the waters of the seven seas could wash away those spots incarnadined.

In the Crucifix is symbolized the perennial crisis in the soul of every man, the choice between the illusory end of time and the imponderable ends of eternity. First are focused all the microscopic conflicts of good and evil that go on in every conscience; or, to put it another way, every man's soul is Calvary written small. That is why the Crucifix is inescapable; we either shrink from it, or we embrace it, but we cannot be indifferent to it. Slinking away from it like a frightened animal is only the dishonest way of saying it is 'self-accusing.'

It is part of that perverse psychology which makes us suit our thinking to the way we live, rather than suiting the way we live to our thinking. There are really only two classes of souls in all the world: those who have the courage to contemplate the Crucifix and the cowards who run from it.

For those who are brave enough to look at the Crucifix, there is a revelation of the moral order — not a moral order based on abstractions, theories, and hypotheses, but a moral order revealed in a Person of absolute goodness who has met the impact of human evil.

It is more like a mirror than a scene, for it reveals not something unrelated to us, but ourselves, our moral beggary, our perversities, and our defeats.

Like nothing else in all the world, it seems to ask the questions: "Where do you stand?" "Which side do you propose to take from this moment on — My side, or the side of moneyed Judas, cowardly Pilate, crafty Annas, or lustful Herod?" We cannot escape an answer.

If on that Cross were someone who himself had been wrong and failed and had compromised with goodness, we could plead an excuse. But here neutrality is impossible because there is no question of something more good or less good — there is only right and wrong.

No answer is the wrong answer. By the answer we give, we judge ourselves. We cannot be on both sides, any more than we can be in Light and Darkness at the same time.

No wonder so many dislike the sight of a Crucifix; no wonder they hate their consciences; no wonder they try to drown its warnings in noise and excitement; no wonder they change the subject of conversation when anyone mentions death, or sneer when they are reminded of sin.

The Cross they can look at, for that might be only a symbol of the contradictions of life; but the Crucifix — they call it 'horrible' when they mean it is accusing.

They may run away from it during life, but they will meet it at the Eternal Judgment, when the Son of Man shall come bearing the Cross in triumph in the clouds of heaven, to render to every man according to his works.

The modern mood of mutilating the Gospel, choosing some texts, and ignoring others, makes men miss the purpose of the life of Christ. He came on earth not primarily to preach, but to redeem. He came less to live than to die.

His mission was not one of mere benevolence, nor to create a revolution in politics or economics, nor to heal, nor to leave a humanitarian ethics — all were these secondary to the one absorbing purpose of His life, the redemption of man.

The sublime declaration of His coming is set down by St. John: "God so loved the world, as to give his only begotten Son; that whosoever believeth in him, may not perish, but may have life everlasting" (John 3:16). Those who regard Christ as no more than a teacher cannot explain either His death or the desire for it.

If a fisherman sitting calmly on a dock throws himself into the sea to prove that he loves his neighbor who is calmly seated beside him, the act is meaningless. But if his neighbor actually fell in and the fisherman jumped into the sea to give up his life to save him, then we should say: "Greater love than this no man hath" (John 15:13).

In like manner, the plunging of Christ into the sea of human suffering is explicable only on the assumption that we were in danger of being drowned by sin. He came to pay a debt and by His obedience in the flesh to expiate our disobedience, and form to Himself a new race of men: He by whom the world was made (Philippians 2: 8-11).

What often happens in the economic order, happened in the moral order; man contracted a bigger debt than he could pay. A sin against Divine Love is greater than man alone can repair.

But if God undertook to forgive the debt through mercy, justice would have been unrequited. God, of course, could pay the debt of man's sin, but He could not in justice; do it apart from man.

A judge will not permit a stranger to walk off the street into a courtroom and take the death sentence of a murderer. In like manner, God could not pay our debt unless He became in some way involved in it.

This the Son of God, Jesus Christ, did by becoming man, assuming a human nature like unto us in all things save sin. He did not merely substitute for us, nor take our place; there is an identification of Him with us. He is the Head of our sin-laden race. In a certain sense, He and we are one Person — the new Adam.

Strictly speaking, Our Lord is man in an absolute sense, not just a man; His humiliation was not so much in assuming a human nature, but in making Himself one with us in the sinful conditions which we created.

He came not into an ideal world, but into this world of sin and suffering — not as a stranger to this life and lot, but as one bearing the burden of the world's sin in Himself, though Himself sinless. He submitted to put on the form and habit of man and to prove His obedience to the Divine Will in the face of temptation, as you and I must do it.

He willed to become the target of the hatred and scorn and mockery of God, and the effect of it was awful, for He faced sin in both its accumulated and massed power and in its experiential delights.

He humbled Himself in taking upon Himself the temporal penal consequences, which are the result of the moral disorder which sin wrought. By His submission to them for our sake He made in Himself the expiation for our sinful nature, becoming, as it were, the living crucible in which the dross of our sinful lives is burned away, that we might be once again pure gold consecrated to God's holy purposes.

It was not that our sins were transferred to Him that we might be guiltless, but that by accepting allegiance with our human nature, He willed to be visited upon Him the conditions which our sins deserved.

Not as a mere man bearing a limited share of the world's burden for sin did He suffer, but as the God-Man whose human suffering embraced within itself the uttermost suffering which sin can bring — physical and mental pain consequent on human mortality; utter self-abnegation for the pride and avarice of men; and defenseless crucifixion for the world's arrogance and brute force.

Thus did He will that in Him our suffering might be transmuted from penalty into expiation, and be the beginning of a new life in Him.

That is why when the hour comes for Him freely to lay down His life; He offers no defense. As a guilty person, He stands before the Judges; silently He listens to the charges and the condemnation; all forces of evil are allowed their free play.

Finally, the Cross was not merely the outbreak of human passion — it was the violent expression of anti-God. It was sin in its essence — the attempted destruction of Divinity.

Sin is self-mutilation, the destruction of personality — when it takes the form of pride, it crowns Goodness with thorns; when it takes the form of dishonesty, it nails hands to a Cross; when it takes the form of hate, it blasphemes the dying; when it takes the form of lust, it crucifies.

Nothing less than bloodshed could have been sin's worst crime and registered sin's deepest hurt.

Evil must work its power to the bitter end, use all its hatred, exhaust all its deceits, unsheathe all of its bloody swords, that being exhausted, Goodness may be revealed as triumphant.

And now that evil was spent in the final act of crucifixion, seeing that in Justice the last farthing was paid in the red coin of His blood and the mortgage against man paid back, He uttered His Cry of Triumph: "It is consummated."

All history, pagan and Jewish, looked forward to this moment; Heaven and earth were separated — now they could be united.

The Pontiff or Bridge-builder has spanned the shores of eternity and time, and the Bridge is the Cross. The last rivet has been put in place; the last nail driven . . . It is consummated.

This is the meaning of a Crucifix: His death is not necessitated by the perverse will of sinful men, and, therefore, is not a martyrdom; but rather a willing submission to their perverse will in order to awaken men to the malignity of their sin and thereby win them over to repentance.

In this one and the same act there stands revealed the awful malignity of sin and the Goodness of God, for it is the Victim who forgives. It was the beauty and loveliness of the God-Man Christ which on the one hand made the crime so great, and on the other hand, made the Divine forgiveness so final and so certain.

That Figure on the Cross bore to the full not only the physical effects of sin which any man might suffer, and not only the mental effects of sin which all of us ought to feel, but the spiritual effects of sin which only He could feel because being sinless, He was not part of it. Only the sinless know the horror of sin.

If you can stand the gaze of a Crucifix long enough, you will discover these truths.

First, if sin cost Him, Who is Innocence, so much, then I who am guilty cannot take it lightly; second, there is only one thing worse in all the world than sin — and that is to forget I am a sinner; third, more bitter than the Crucifixion must be my rejection of that Love by which I was redeemed.

Every law, physical or moral, has its penalties. If I disobey the law of health, nature penalizes me with sickness. If I disobey the moral law, I cannot eternally hope to escape its consequences as though I had not violated it.

Some time may intervene between the sowing and the harvest, the wheat and the cockle may be permitted to grow together; but there one day comes the day of judgment when the wheat is gathered into barns, and the cockle is burned.

Suppose now you admitted that you were a sinner, and you wished to be justified by that Redemption. How would you put the two together? How would you tie up a sinful heart with that Cross? How span 1900 years to make Redemption effective in you — now at this hour? This is a very practical question and merits an answer.

It would be easy to answer if that Cross could be lifted out of the rocks of Calvary by some giant hand and set down in the very midst of our cities and in the center of our plains.

Suppose such a miracle actually happened, so that instead of looking back in memory and imagination to Calvary as something that happened we could see Calvary re-enacted before our very eyes, so truly and really that we could gain the same merit as if we stood on Good Friday beneath the shadow of the Cross.

Suppose in some visible way we could "show the death of the Lord until he come" (1 Corinthians 11:26), that we might incorporate ourselves to it as Mary and John did on Calvary.

We have a right to expect that the Memorial of His Passion be prolonged to this hour, for did He not give that Memorial the night before He died by consecrating bread and wine into His own body and blood, and tell His Apostles to do it in memory of Him?

If that Redemptive Death could be so visibly re-enacted in our days of war and woe and misery, then the Cross would not be a memory, but an action; not a prayer but a renewed sacrifice; not a thing unrelated to us, but something made available for our participation.

It almost sounds too good to be true. But that is precisely what has happened! For Catholics, the Mass is Calvary renewed! On the Cross He was alone; in the Mass, we are with Him. In that sense, Christ is still on the Cross.

THE SEVENTH VIRTUE

- Charity -

"Father, into thy hands I commend my spirit."

CHARITY IS THE PERFECTION of Justice. As Aristotle put it so wisely: "Where Justice is, there is a further need of friendship; but where friendship is, there is no need of justice." Complementing that last thought, St. Augustine said: "Love God and do whatever you please," for if you love God, you will never do anything to offend Him.

It was, therefore, fitting that the Sixth Word, reflecting the Justice of God which fulfilled the will of the Father in its smallest detail, should be followed by the Seventh Word of Charity: "Father, into Thy Hands I commend My Spirit." It was like the seventh day of Creation. During the six words, the Son of God labored forgiving enemies, pardoning thieves, solacing a mother, atoning for faithlessness, pleading for love, atoning for injustice, and now He takes His rest and goes back home.

Love is to a great extent a stranger on earth; it finds momentary satisfactions in human hearts, but it soon becomes restless. It was born of the Infinite and can never be satisfied with anything less. In a certain sense, God spoiled us for any other love except Himself, because He made us out of His Divine Love.

Born of His Everlasting Fire, the earthly sparks of affection can but kindle our hearts. We are all kings in exile; prodigals from the Father's House. As flames must mount upward to the sun, so He Who came from the Father must go back again to the Father: Love must return to Love. "Father, into Thy Hands I commend My Spirit."

It is noteworthy that He said these words with a loud voice. No one was taking His life away. It was not like the love expressed by a dying parent to his child; such love is begotten of a heart meeting the impact of the inevitable. But in the case of Our Lord, it was completely and absolutely unforced — the deliverance of freedom.

Thus did He teach us that all love on this earth involves choice. When, for example, a young man expresses his love to a young woman and asks her to become his wife, he is not just making an affirmation of love; he is also negating his love for anyone else. In that one act by which he chooses her, he rejects all that is not her.

There is no other real way in which to prove we love a thing than by choosing it in preference to something else. Words and sighs of love may be, and often are, expressions of egotism or passion; but deeds are proofs of love.

When God put Adam and Eve in the garden, the preservation of their gifts was conditioned upon fidelity to Him. But how prove fidelity except by choice, namely by obeying God's Will in preference to any other will.

In the freedom of choosing a fruit to a garden, was hidden the test of their love. By their decision, they proved they loved something else more than God.

After the Resurrection, Our Lord prefaced the conferring of the powers of jurisdiction on Peter as the Rock of the Church, by asking the question: "Simon, Son of John, lovest thou Me more than these?" Three times the question is asked because three times Peter had denied Our Lord — Once again, love is tested by preference.

The beginning and the end of the public life of Our Lord reveals this same basic quality of love. On the Mount of Temptation and on the Mount of Calvary, Satan and wicked men throw bribes into the balance to influence His choice. Surveying all the grandeur of earth, Satan in a frightening boast said: "All these kingdoms are mine." He offered them all to Our Lord if falling down He would adore him. Jesus could have the world if He would give up heaven.

Now on the other mount, it is satanic men who tempt as they shout: "Come Down and we will believe." "Come Down from your belief in the Heavenly Father." "Come Down from your belief in Divinity." "Come Down from the cross and we will believe." Jesus could have believers if He would give up the Cross, but without the Cross, Jesus could not be the Saviour.

But as He did not fall down before Satan, neither did He come down from the cross, for perfect love is the choice of Divine Love. He would choose the Father's Will either to this wealth or His bodily comfort. And that is why: "Greater love than this no man hath, that he lay down His life for his friend."

Now His love was not just declared by word, but proven by deed. He could enjoy the fruit of perfect love: "Father, into Thy Hands I commend My Spirit."

For us, there can be but one conclusion: it is not enough to bear a Christian name, we must also merit the name. "Not everyone that saith 'Lord, Lord' shall enter into the Kingdom of heaven." We can prove we love Our Lord only by choosing Him in preference to anything else. The condition of returning to the Father's hands on the last day is the choice of His Cross and all that it implies.

At any moment of our existence, we can test whether we are truly Christian, and that test will be the obedience to His commandments: "He that hath my commandments and keepeth them, he it is that loveth me. And he that loveth me shall be loved of my Father, and I will love him and manifest myself to him. And my Father will love him, and we will come to him and make our abode with him" (John 14: 21-23).

This brings us to the second lesson of Charity. In this Seventh Word, Our Lord did not express Love of the Father in terms of keeping commandments: it was a personal relationship; that of Father and Son. Even in the text: "He that loveth my commandments and keepeth them, he it is that loveth me," the possessive adjective is to be noted. The commandments are not abstract laws separable from His Person; they are one with Him.

"If you love Me keep My commandments." Perfect love is therefore quite distinct from obedience to commandments as laws. Laws are for the imperfect; love is for the perfect. Law is for those who want to know the minimum; love is for those who are interested in the maximum. Laws, therefore, are generally negative: "Thou shalt not . . ."; love is affirmative: "Love the Lord, thy God, with thy whole heart."

Imperfect Christians are concerned only with keeping the laws of the Church; they want to know how far they can go without committing a mortal sin; how near they can get to hell without falling in; how much wrong they can do short of punishment; how they can please God without displeasing themselves.

The perfect Christian is never interested in borders, or the minimum because love is never measured. Mary Magdalene did not count out the drops of the precious ointment as she poured them on the feet of Our Divine Saviour. Judas did; he counted the cost.

But Magdalene, because she loved, broke the vessel and gave everything, for love has no limits. St. Paul, in like manner, could think of no better way of describing the love of Christ for sinners than to say: "He emptied himself."

There is no law that those who love should give gifts to their beloved; there are no laws that mothers should love children. Where there is love, there is no law, because love has no limits.

There was no boundary to the cross; the arms outstretched even into infinity portrayed the universal efficacy of Redemption. There was no counting the cost: "Not my will but Thine be done." He even refused to touch a drink which might have dulled His senses, and thus deprive His will of complete self-devotion for men.

Like Magdalene, He broke the chalice of His Life, and poured out "plentiful Redemption." Such perfect love could be compensated only by a return to perfect love: "Father, into Thy Hands I commend My Spirit."

The essence of Christianity is love, yes! But not love as our world understands it; not loving those who love us, but loving even those who hate us. Love is not in the organism, but in the will; not in affection, but in intention; not in satisfaction, but in preference to the choosing of God above everything.

Every soul then, even those who irritate, annoy and hate us must be looked upon as a potential lover of Christ, and every Christian must be regarded as a kind of consecrated host.

The most degraded man on the face of the earth is precious, and Christ died for Him. That poor soul may have made the wrong choice, but that is not for us to decide. While he has life, he has hope. He might not seem lovable to us, but he is loved by God.

The perfection of all virtue is charity; love of God and love of our neighbor. Whether or not we, like Christ, shall deliver our soul into the Father's hands on the last day, depends entirely upon the use we make of our freedom.

When we abuse it, our conscience tells us that we are our own worst enemy. "Now I know that when I nailed thee to a Cross, it was my own heart I slew." All sin is self-mutilation.

Most of us are kept back from a perfect love of God, "... fearful lest having Him, we should have naught else beside." There is a fear of losing something by obedience to Him; a hesitation of venturing all on God. Could we but see that when we have the sun we need not the candle, then all would be easy.

God grant us the light to see that in loving Him we have everything, and with that light, the grace to die with His words on our lips: "Father, into Thy Hands I commend My Spirit."

ACKNOWLEDGMENTS

To the members of the Archbishop Fulton John Sheen Foundation in Peoria, Illinois. In particular, to the Most Rev. Daniel R. Jenky, C.S.C., Bishop of Peoria, for your leadership and fidelity to the cause of Sheen's canonization and the creation of this book.

www.archbishopsheencause.org

To the volunteers at the Archbishop Fulton J. Sheen Mission Society of Canada: your motto "Unless Souls are Saved, Nothing is Saved", speaks to the reality that Jesus Christ came into the world to make salvation available to all souls.

www.archbishopfultonjsheenmissionsocietyofcanada.org

To the staff at Sophia Institute Press for their invaluable assistance in sharing the writings of Archbishop Fulton J. Sheen to a new generation of readers.

www.sophiainstitute.com

To the good folks at 'Bishop Sheen Today'. We value your guidance, support, and prayers in helping us to share the wisdom of Archbishop Fulton J. Sheen. Your apostolic work of sharing his audio and video presentations along with his many writings to a worldwide audience is very much appreciated.

www.bishopsheentoday.com

And lastly, to Archbishop Fulton J. Sheen, whose teachings on Our Lord's Passion and His Seven Last Words continue to inspire me to love God more and to appreciate the gift of the Church. May we be so blessed as to imitate Archbishop Sheen's love for the saints, the sacraments, the Eucharist, and the Blessed Virgin Mary. May the Good Lord grant him a very high place in heaven!

ABOUTH THE AUTHOR
Fulton J. Sheen
(1895–1979)

ARCHBISHOP SHEEN, best known for his popularly televised and syndicated television program, Life is Worth Living, is held today as one of Catholicism's most widely recognized figures of the twentieth century.

Fulton John Sheen, born May 8, 1895, in El Paso, Illinois was raised and educated in the Roman Catholic faith. Originally named Peter John Sheen, he came to be known as a young boy by his mother's maiden name, Fulton. He was ordained a priest of the Diocese of Peoria at St. Mary's Cathedral in Peoria, IL on September 20, 1919.

Following his ordination, Sheen studied at the Catholic University of Louvain, where he earned a doctorate in philosophy in 1923. That same year, he received the Cardinal Mercier Prize for International Philosophy, becoming the first-ever American to earn this distinction.

Upon returning to America, after varied and extensive work throughout Europe, Sheen continued to preach and teach theology and philosophy from 1927 to 1950, at the Catholic University of America in Washington D.C.

Beginning in 1930, Sheen hosted a weekly Sunday night radio broadcast called 'The Catholic Hour'. This broadcast captured many devoted listeners, reportedly drawing an audience of four million people every week for over twenty years.

In 1950, he became the National Director of the Society for the Propagation of the Faith, raising funds to support missionaries. During the sixteen years that he held this position, millions of dollars were raised to support the missionary activity of the Church. These efforts influenced tens of millions of people all over the world, bringing them to know Christ and his Church. In addition, his preaching and personal example brought about many converts to Catholicism.

In 1951, Sheen was appointed Auxiliary Bishop of the Archdiocese of New York. That same year, he began hosting his television program 'Life is Worth Living', which lasted for six years.

In the course of its run, that program competed for airtime with popular television programs hosted by the likes of Frank Sinatra and Milton Berle. Sheen's program held its own, and in 1953, just two years after its debut, he won an Emmy Award for "Most Outstanding Television Personality." Fulton Sheen credited the Gospel writers - Matthew, Mark, Luke, and John - for their valuable contribution to his success. Sheen's television show ran until 1957, boasting as many as thirty million weekly viewers.

In the Fall of 1966, Sheen was appointed Bishop of Rochester, New York. During that time, Bishop Sheen hosted another television series, 'The Fulton Sheen Program' which ran from 1961 to 1968, closely modeling the format of his 'Life is Worth Living' series.

After nearly three years as Bishop of Rochester, Fulton Sheen resigned and was soon appointed by Pope Paul VI as Titular Archbishop of the See of Newport, Wales. This new appointment allowed Sheen the flexibility to continue preaching.

Another claim to fame was Bishop Sheen's annual Good Friday homilies, which he preached for fifty-eight consecutive years at St. Patrick's Cathedral in New York City, and elsewhere. Sheen also led numerous retreats for priests and religious, preaching at conferences all over the world.

When asked by Pope St. Pius XII how many converts he had made, Sheen responded, "Your Holiness, I have never counted them. I am always afraid that if I did count them, I might think I made them, instead of the Lord."

Sheen was known for being approachable and down to earth. He used to say, "If you want people to stay as they are, tell them what they want to hear. If you want to improve them, tell them what they should know." This he did, not only in his preaching but also through his numerous books and articles. His book titled 'Peace of Soul' was sixth on the New York Times best-seller list.

Three of Sheen's great loves were: the missions and the propagation of the faith; the Holy Mother of God and the Eucharist.

He made a daily holy hour of prayer before the Blessed Sacrament. It was from Jesus Himself that he drew strength and inspiration to preach the gospel, and in the Presence of Whom that he prepared his homilies. "I beg [Christ] every day to keep me strong physically and alert mentally, in order to preach His gospel and proclaim His Cross and Resurrection," he said. "I am so happy doing this that I sometimes feel that when I come to the good Lord in Heaven, I will take a few days' rest and then ask Him to allow me to come back again to this earth to do some more work."

His contributions to the Catholic Church are numerous and varied, ranging from educating in classrooms, churches, and homes, to preaching over a nationally-publicized radio show, and two television programs, as well as penning over sixty written works. Archbishop Fulton J. Sheen had a gift for communicating the Word of God in the most pure, simple way. His strong background in philosophy helped him to relate to everyone in a highly personalized manner. His timeless messages continue to have great relevance today. His goal was to inspire everyone to live a God-centered life with the joy and love that God intended.

On October 2, 1979, Archbishop Sheen received his greatest accolade, when Pope St. John Paul II embraced him at St. Patrick's Cathedral in New York City. The Holy Father said to him, "You have written and spoken well of the Lord Jesus. You are a loyal son of the Church."

The good Lord called Fulton Sheen home on December 9, 1979. His television broadcasts now available through various media, and his books, extend his earthly work of winning souls for Christ. Sheen's cause for canonization was opened in 2002. In 2012, Pope Benedict XVI declared him 'Venerable', and in July of 2019, Pope Francis formally approved the miracle necessary for Sheen's beatification and canonization process to move forward. The time and date for the church to declare Archbishop Fulton J. Sheen a saint is in God's hands.

Books Available Through Bishop Sheen Today Publishing

The Rainbow of Sorrow

The Seven Last Words

Calvary and the Mass

Love One Another

The Cross and the Beatitudes

The Cross and the Crisis

Love One Another

Victory Over Vice

The Seven Virtues

For God and Country

God and War

The Divine Verdict

God Love You

The Seven Last Words Explained

The Priest Is Not His Own

The Cross and the Crib

Philosophies at War

The Seven Last Words of Christ Explained

Father, Forgive Them for They Know Not What They Do.

This Day Thou Shall Be with Me in Paradise

Woman Behold Your Son; Behold Your Mother

My God! My God! Why Hast Thou Forsaken Me?

I Thirst

It is Finished

Father Into Your Hands I Commend My Spirit

Liberty, Equality and Fraternity

Missions and the World Crisis

Seven Words to the Cross

Seven Pillars of Peace

The Holy Hour Prayer Book

Seven Words of Jesus & Mary

www.bishopsheentoday.com

www.ingramcontent.com/pod-product-compliance
Lightning Source LLC
Chambersburg PA
CBHW021614120626
46545CB00001B/223